Praise for *Risk*

"I've always been an adrenaline junkie, so *Risk* instantly appealed to me. This book goes beyond the interesting and engaging *descriptive stories* to provide much needed *prescriptive insight* to enable men to live more boldly and powerfully. If you're up for being challenged in significant ways, read this book."

—MARK SANBORN, president of Sanborn and Associates Inc. and author of *The Fred Factor: How Passion in Your Work and Life Can Turn the Ordinary into the Extraordinary*

"Shocking are the Scripture's stories of men that took risks! So are the modern-day accounts of men changing the world for God by taking risks. And then there's you… Are you risking it? This is a man's book for men—men of God ready to rip into the ends of the age. Dive into *Risk!*"

—DR. WAYNE CORDEIRO, senior pastor of New Hope Christian Fellowship Oahu and author of *Doing Church as a Team* and *Culture Shift*

"*Risk* is a book for men. It challenges us to faith, courage, and commitment. Kenny Luck tells the inspiring stories of men who risked everything to follow God. Don't miss this exciting and riveting challenge. It will stir your soul to action."

—DR. JERRY FALWELL, Liberty University in Lynchburg, Virginia

"*Risk* is a must-read for any man seeking significant change in his life. This book has great depth and momentum. Kenny Luck clearly communicates the message of what it means to completely sell out to God. Thank you Kenny. I pray that all men everywhere will take the risk and trust God with everything."

—DAVEY BUHL, director of men's ministry at Christ Church at Grove Farm

"I always want to know if the author of a book exemplifies what he has written. Kenny Luck certainly does! He has taken the risk to leave what seemed more comfortable and secure in order to follow God's call in his life. *Risk: Are You Willing to Trust God with Everything?* invites men everywhere to do the same. It is a book that is not afraid to confront the realities, to challenge the heart, and to celebrate the joy that are a part of the risk of faith."

—TOM HOLLADAY, teaching pastor at Saddleback Church and author of *Foundations: 11 Core Truths to Build Your Life On*

"*Risk* is my kind of book, and Kenny Luck is my kind of guy. Jesus lived risking everything, and this book inspires you and me to live like Jesus lived and to do what Jesus did. Warning: *Risk* is for the courageous, not cowards. Be bold! Buy *Risk!* Live it!"

—WALT KALLESTAD, author of *Entrepreneurial Faith; A Passionate Life; The Passionate Church;* and *Turn Your Church Inside Out;* and senior pastor of Community Church of Joy in Glendale, Arizona

"Kenny brings a fresh challenge to every Christian man by stepping up and accepting the risks of speaking out for God. As a pastor, I get the joy of seeing how this message lives out weekly through our men at Saddleback Church. It's not theory, but real! Kenny's passion and calling is making a difference!"

—DOUG SLAYBAUGH, president of Purpose Driven

"*Risk* challenges the heart of the many issues that men are dealing with today. Kenny has done a thorough job of meeting men where they are and giving us a game plan to be men of God. I highly recommend that all men read *Risk* and allow the encouragements to saturate their lives."

—GREG SURRATT, senior pastor of Seacoast Church

risk

Are you willing to trust God with everything?

kenny luck

WATERBROOK
PRESS

RISK
PUBLISHED BY WATERBROOK PRESS
12265 Oracle Boulevard, Suite 200
Colorado Springs, Colorado 80921
A division of Random House Inc.

Details in some anecdotes and stories have been changed to protect the identities of the persons involved.

ISBN 1-57856-986-9

Library of Congress Cataloging-in-Publication Data
Luck, Kenneth L., 1964–
Risk : are you willing to trust God with everything? / Kenny Luck.— 1st ed.
p. cm.
ISBN 1-57856-986-9
1. Trust in God. 2. Faith. 3. Christian life. 4. Risk. I. Title.
BV4637.L83 2006
248.8'42—dc22

2006005748

Printed in the United States of America
2006—First Edition

10 9 8 7 6 5 4 3 2 1

risk

This book is dedicated to my brothers around the world who are being persecuted for their faith in Jesus Christ. These are the men the world may never know and the same men of whom the world is not worthy. We suffer with you, my brothers, remember you, and seek your deliverance. You are our inspiration and example.

contents

acknowledgments

I would like to express my deep gratitude to a few sets of people who risk taking chances on a goofball like me, beginning with my pastor, Rick Warren. Thank you for trusting me to care for the men of Saddleback and providing me with an example of one who risks greatly for the kingdom. It is an honor to follow you into battle. Few pastors lead with such integrity and transparency. I know I speak for millions around the globe whose lives have been changed because you continue to seek the Lord and never settle for less than the global glory of God.

To the Herd, the men of Saddleback: Thank you for your dedication to being God's men and adventuring with me as God calls us to lead personally, locally, and globally. You never fail to inspire me by how far you are taking your faith. Never stop.

I would also like to acknowledge and thank Danny Wallen and Tom Chapin at Every Man Ministries who refuse to let me plateau as a leader and who have the courage and commitment to stretch me (however painfully) so that I can lead out of character. Thank you for pushing me to take the greatest risk of all—not settling as a man and seeking more of Christ's character with each step of my journey.

On the writing side I would like to thank my mentor and coach, Mike Yorkey, whose hand in my development will be felt in every work I will ever have the privilege to write. Steve Arterburn and Fred Stoeker deserve equal credit for their dedication and influence in my journey. And to the team at WaterBrook Press who sat with me and listened to the vision for this series of books and had the guts to risk adventuring with me. Specifically, I need to thank Don Pape, Steve Cobb, Ginia Hairston, Dudley Delffs, Bruce Nygren, and Mick Silva for their help and support. I am very fortunate to serve the Lord with all of you.

On the most personal level, thank you, Chrissy, for risking your heart on me. I am still on top of the world almost eighteen years later.

chapter 1

inner turbulence

The only adequate answer to an aggressively pagan world is for Christians to recover the New Testament power of spiritual aggression.

—KARL BARTH

"I am firing myself."

The chairman of our company returned my statement with a blank stare. My professional freefall had begun. It picked up even more speed when the second most frightening sentence I have ever uttered escaped my mouth.

"I sense God calling me to work with men on a full-time basis." I didn't know exactly what it looked like, but I wanted to help churches connect their men and grow strong men's communities.

Yet again, no response.

A voice in my head filled the silence. *That sounded even more stupid than firing yourself… In fact, it was idiotic. This little ministry venture of yours will cause major problems for your wife.*

Man, was *that* true! Before I knew it, I was in a war zone, fireworks of fear exploding in my head.

- Boom! *You are the CEO of your company with 265 great employees.*
- Kaboom! *Annual revenues hit eight million this year.*
- Pop! Pop! *You've worked your way to the top over the last nine years, from a marketing assistant to running the show!*
- Bang! *You have a robust 401(k) deal going and are fully vested.*
- Waboom! *You have a deferred compensation package that guarantees you thousands of extra dollars per year if you'll just stay with the company.*
- Shabang! *You have stock options.*
- And for the finale! *Chrissy is feeling financially secure for the first time in twelve years of marriage! After spending the last few years becoming debt free, do you really want to press the nuclear hot button of your marriage?*

Then the counterthought: *You know what you need to do. You just have to get off your blessed assurance and do it.*

Oh yeah, I forgot about that, Lord—The soldier who dropped that God-bomb on me was my pastor. The day before, his words had come thundering from heaven, waking me out of my stupor. After a year of debating God's call about when to start my nonprofit ministry, the answer had come. I had been praying for clarity, and now, finally, here it was, clear as day, in bright, fluorescent green.

But where was that confidence *now?* Instead of feeling like Elwood from the Blues Brothers "on a mission from God," I felt more like Minnie Mouse and my fingernail polish didn't match my skirt, if you know what I mean.

Then my boss's mouth finally opened. "Kenny," he began. *Oh, mama. Here it comes.* "I am so excited for you. What can I do to help you with this transition?" I stood there paralyzed, unable to respond. "Well," he said, answering his own question, "since you've been with the company for nine years, I can make sure you get a nine-month severance. And if you want, you can house your new venture out of the corporate office rent free."

The soldier who dropped that God-bomb on me was my pastor.

Holy #%$! I mean, cannoli!*

Well, I used that severance to help launch Every Man Ministries (EMM) in the spring of 2000. God is using the EMM team to help spark a revolution in men's ministry, spiritually freeing hundreds of thousands of men and igniting the church worldwide through conferences, campaigns, pastors' trainings, books, and resources.

Charles Spurgeon expressed, for all men who dare to be obedient, the untold power of a small decision for God when he observed, "We do not know all that we are doing when we risk for our faith. Great wheels turn on little axles." Yes, my brotha! I had no idea how big a small decision to do what God was asking me to do would be for my own life, and eventually for countless other men.

Ditching the "Safe" Life

Predictability. Control. Safety. Comfort.

The book in your hands is about exploring God's feelings on how those subjects fit, or better yet, *don't* fit in your quest toward becoming God's man. In fact, when you look at this climber graphic behind text, that's a signal to pause and consider ways to apply the principles of risk in your own life.

As with all God's men, the first disciples had their own "Oh, mama" moments with Christ. Each was on a journey to fulfill God's purposes for his life. Aware of this, Jesus knew he had to address the whole issue of risky commitment if the disciples were to succeed in their mission after He'd conquered the Cross. He was direct and uncomfortably honest:

> Then Jesus began to tell them that he, the Son of Man, would suffer many terrible things and be rejected by the leaders, the leading priests, and the teachers of religious law. He would be killed, and three days later he would rise again. As he talked about this openly with his disciples, Peter took him aside and told him he shouldn't say things like that.
>
> Jesus turned and looked at his disciples and then said to Peter very sternly, "Get away from me, Satan! You are seeing things merely from a human point of view, not from God's."
>
> Then he called his disciples and the crowds to come over and listen. "If any of you wants to be my follower," he told them, "you must put aside your selfish ambition, shoulder your cross, and fol-

> low me. If you try to keep your life for yourself, you will lose it. But if you give up your life for my sake and for the sake of the Good News, you will find true life." (Mark 8:31–35, NLT)

Satan had already tried to sabotage Jesus at the outset of His ministry through promises of pleasure and power and protection. Jesus heard him again trying to lie to Peter. Real spiritual warfare surrounds every good man He wants to use. So He got real. He told Peter and His disciples exactly what was going on. He wanted them and us to know the very real risks we take to follow Him. It means giving up the life you may have expected you'd live to live the one God *calls* you to live.

Take risks for Me and you will find life. Hedge your bet and you will lose it all.

What's more, Jesus makes it clear to His men that all the energy they might spend trying to eliminate risk would actually work against His purposes in their lives. Jesus knew that very shortly the chips would be down for His guys, and the only true option would be to bet it all. It could not have been a more desperate situation, so He made it plain: Take risks for Me and you will find life. Hedge your bet and you will lose it all.

Jumping into Risk

Tension. Unpredictability. Letting go. Adrenaline.

Oh yeah, baby. Jumping off of things is in our DNA. It took me about two seconds to come up with my short list of things I used to love jumping off. The roof into a cold pool. Trampolines. The swings. A pogo stick to Billy Joel music, eight hundred and fifty seven times in my parents' garage. Over Calabasas Creek with my yellow Schwinn. Into mischief for the simple thrill of it.

How about you?

Our fathers or mothers looked at us and said, "What were you thinking?" We said, "I don't know." And that was the truth: there *was* no explanation! We were boys. We were stretching the limits of our courage, testing the limits of our abilities, risking injury for the rush of what was on the other side of the experience. We lived for that freedom and risked life and limb naturally. What a great life purpose!

What qualities would you as a man need to recapture from your boyhood to shape your masculinity in Christ right now?

It's not a mystery that Jesus used a little boy to answer the spiritual-significance question: "Who's the greatest in the kingdom of heaven?" Imagine being a first-century man looking on, wondering the same thing: "What can I do here that will make me significant up there with God?" Jesus looked at His guys and knew exactly what message to send.

> He called a little child and had him stand among them. And he said: "I tell you the truth, unless you change and become like little children, you will never enter the kingdom of heaven. Therefore, whoever humbles himself like this child is the greatest in the kingdom of heaven." (Matthew 18:2–4)

What would this mean to you? What qualities would you as a man need to recapture from your boyhood to shape your masculinity in Christ right now?

Eager to trust. Eager to risk. Eager to "jump off."

Risk is in the DNA of every man, put there by God and for God. You may have misplaced it, neglected it, misused it, but it is time to get it back. It is time to do something great for God with it *right now.* This means committing to the four principles of RISK for every God's man. Here they come…

Right View of God

Is He or isn't He? God, that is. Sounds silly but I am dead serious. Both the root of our fears and our courage to risk hinge on our view of God. A. W. Tozer was on the mark about us when he said, "Were we to extract from any man a complete answer to the question, 'What comes into your mind when you think about God?' we might predict with certainty the spiritual future of that man." It makes perfect sense. The most important thing about us is our concept of God.

Is He omnipotent or impotent? sovereign and aloof? omnipresent and available? high and lifted up or familiar? punitive or kind? faithful or flaky? loving or vengeful? just or unjust? able or unable to make a difference? creator or kill-joy?

Little God? Little risk.
Little love for God?
Little love for people.

When our concept of Him is diminished, so is courage for Him. But if our concept is correct, we become unstoppable for the kingdom. So how big is your God? The answer to that lies not in your words but in the substance of your actions for Him. If you know He is who He says He is, you will risk big. Little God? Little risk. Little love for God? Little love for people. The connections are endless.

Your concept of God is so important that when it is off, you suffer, your relationships suffer, and your mission for God in the world suffers. Wrong notions rot moral courage. Right notions produce radical actions. In fact, no man's life *for* God will ever outperform his view *of* God. That is why Jesus feared no man. He saw His Father clearly and lived confidently.

> They came to him and said, "Teacher, we know you are a man of integrity. *You aren't swayed by men, because you pay no attention to who they are;* but you teach the way of God in accordance with the truth." (Mark 12:14, emphasis added)

What about for you? No person, no obstacle, no dream, no problem, no fear, and no issue in your life is bigger than your God. If He wants something to happen, *nothing* can stop it. And if it doesn't happen at all or the way you envisioned, His purpose will be worked out another way. Brother, that's freedom! You cannot lose. His faithfulness and purpose will *always* prevail. If you see God for who He is, you will gamble hard on His way, just like Jesus did.

As we start to think about risking more for God, we have to guard our minds against thoughts that diminish the reality of His majesty and power.

Identity Settled

When you know who you are, taking big risks makes sense.

> But you, *man of God,* flee from all this, and pursue righteousness, godliness, faith, love, endurance and gentleness. *Fight* the good fight of the faith. *Take hold* of the eternal life to which you were called when you made your good confession in the presence of many witnesses. (1 Timothy 6:11–12, emphasis added)

Paul knew that the quickest and most effective way to pull greatness out of his pupil Timothy was to remind him of who he *really* was. He might be tempted to pretend to be someone else, but Timothy was God's man—that was his identity. His mentor knew that his identity shaped his loyalty and that loyalty is what drives our choices. In Timothy's life it meant fleeing inconsistent identities, fighting hard for what he believed, and being loyal to his calling as God's man.

If we call Him Lord, Lord, we will risk it all to do what He says.

In the same way, Jesus pulled His guys in tight to emphasize that their identity meant lining up on the right side of the ball. "If you belonged to the world," He said, "it would love you as its own. As it is, you do not belong to the world, but *I have chosen you out of the world.* That is why the world hates you" (John 15:19, emphasis added). The crystal clear message: blending in with the world is not the mark of His men.

Here's a spiritual fact: we risk more for God when our identity is firmly *in God.* Today, His Spirit is confronting all His men everywhere with the same question: "Are you on *this* team?" Jesus made a habit of confronting guys posing as believers (as opposed to risking as believers) by asking: "Why do you call me 'Lord, Lord,' and do not do what I say?" (Luke 6:46). In other words, "Identify with Me fully; don't just pay lip service."

No faking it. Flip the question over and you get the solution: if we call Him Lord, Lord, we will risk it all to do what He says. And every time we choose Christ, our identity becomes more deeply imbedded in Him.

To risk more for Christ we need to be squarely in Christ. No wavering. So decide now where your identity and loyalty will lie if you want to experience maximum connection with God and His purposes.

Sacrifice Like Christ

These famous words of martyred missionary Jim Elliot make him the patron saint of spiritual guts in my book: "He is no fool who gives up what he cannot keep in order to gain what he cannot lose." In a single sentence he captures the essence of what it means to risk spiritually. At some point we stop caring about earth in order to populate and invest in heaven. In Elliot's case, he traded his bride, his career, and ultimately his very breath for Jesus' sake and for the sake of the gospel. He lost his life to gain his life. His talk of sacrifice was matched by a life of sacrifice.

And while few of us will be called to give our lives, millions of us will be called to sacrifice our wills for His will, material wealth for spiritual wealth, earthly recognition for heavenly recognition, carnal appetites for godly appetites, career dreams for God's dream, corporate ladders for family health, and convenient compromise for spiritual integrity. Sacrifice and suffering loss for the sake of our faith is what connects the God-Man and God's man.

> In bringing many sons to glory [your name implied here], it was fitting that God, for whom and through whom everything exists, should make the author of their salvation perfect through suffering.

> Both the one who makes men holy and those who are made holy are of the same family. So Jesus is not ashamed to call them brothers. (Hebrews 2:10–11)

Jesus was made fit to lead us through suffering. Naturally, if He lives in you, God will continue to make you fit to lead by calling *you* to a sacrificial life. More important, sacrifice *for* Christ is what unites you most deeply *with* Christ. How else could the apostle Paul write, "I want to know Christ and the power of his resurrection and *the fellowship of sharing in his sufferings*" (Philippians 3:10, emphasis added)?

Risking for God is synonymous with sacrificing for God, and it is not a burden; it is a privilege as God's man. It is a special bond we share with Christ and part of our worship. We lay our lives on the altar so He can use us mightily for His work.

Men who dare greatly for their faith have asked and answered this question: *Am I willing to sacrifice my agenda in order to be used for God's agenda?*

Kingdom-Build

When your view of God is right, your identity as God's man is settled (as in, no more competing identities), and you are willing to sacrifice your agenda for His service, it's time to build something that will outlast you. It's time to invest in something you can't take with you but something you can send ahead to eternity. It's time to get busy building the kingdom of God right where you live, in your local church, and in your world. It's time to start thinking outside the box and dream—dream big God dreams.

The kingdom doesn't need more religious guys. It requires more big, hairy, audacious dreamers. Think I'm playing you? Listen to Jesus describe the kind of man God uses for breakthrough works of His Spirit in the world. Could He be talking about you?

> From the days of John the Baptist until now, the kingdom of heaven has been forcefully advancing, and *forceful men* lay hold of it. (Matthew 11:12, emphasis added)

As soon as John started talking about a Messiah, the battle line was drawn. Men throughout the centuries have been challenged to cross that line, out of comfort and into risk for their King. Forceful men have been moved from within with God's vision for kingdom expansion. And even today, forceful men still hunger and thirst for the kingdom of God to explode in people's hearts wherever they may be. The kingdom mentality is not for the spiritually timid; it is for the man of war. And it *is* about winning—souls, communities, people in desperation, countries in darkness, and all the particular battles of your world. It's about winning men you know to join forces and affect the course of history.

I had a missionary from Kenya write me recently about the AIDS and orphan epidemic in his country. His assessment on the ground gave me a glimpse of the global impact men have and a template for the solution in many cultures: "Here in Kenya," he said, "we don't have an AIDS problem; we have a man problem." He went on to describe how migrant labor forces men to seek work in cities far from home: they sleep with prostitutes, then come back and infect their villages with the virus. He begged me to come and join him to bring men's ministry rather than medicine. Africa needs men who make things better, not men who make messes—Africa needs leaders.

He finished by saying, "If men start making different moral choices, the country will change." How many other communities around the world could say the same thing?

From leading nations to providing for families, men are needed to plant churches, equip future leaders, assist the poor, care for the sick, and educate the next generation. A vast army is being raised, and troops are being delivered to global hotspots in record numbers. For example, Rick Warren's Global PEACE Plan network is mobilizing one billion believers to "go" as Jesus commanded and slay these global giants. The deployment has already begun. Over the next couple of decades it will be the most powerful show of force the church has mounted in history. And men will be at the center of this movement. The biggest needs will be met not by politicians, by the United Nations, or by throwing money to poor countries. They will be met by God's people. Rick believes, as I do, that our team has the widest and best distribution network in the world—it's called the church. And the world is waiting for its redeemers (little *r*) who can tell the good news of the Redeemer. Men will be the tip of the spear on many fronts of this titanic kingdom advance.

Over the next couple of decades it will be the most powerful show of force the church has mounted in history. And men will be at the center of this movement.

Will *you* be in play?

Stepping Off Spiritual Ledges

"Dad," Ryan said, "Jenna wants to jump off."

"What?"

"She said she wants to jump into the ocean."

Disbelieving, I asked Jenna myself to shake her into reality. "Jenna, you want to jump off *that* ledge with *me* into the ocean?"

"Yep." It seemed desire trumped dissuasion. Ryan and I were having too much fun to resist, she was watching, and there was no height requirement.

"Great! Let's go," I said, half expecting her to bail out once she looked down.

Not a chance.

The drop into the ocean was seven times higher than my little princess was tall. And I need to emphasize "princess." Jenna's world is that of Polly Pocket, Groovy Girl dolls, ballet, art class, and Dora the Explorer—not dropping into quarter pipes like her older brother or diving into the ocean from a twenty-foot ledge. Jenna's previous record height was two feet of elevation in a backyard pool. So for *her,* this was a titanic leap into the deep blue.

> *"I kept telling myself everything will be all right because I am with my dad."*

"One. Two. Three. Go!" On the "Go!" signal Jenna jumped off, dropped twenty feet straight down in all of one and a half seconds, and then plunged five feet underwater. After surfacing, she used her first breath to exclaim with a huge smile, "That was fun, let's do it again." Of course, right?

This became more than a cute story or proud parenting moment as we climbed that ladder out of the ocean and started walking up the stairs for round two when I asked her, "So what were you feeling before you jumped off, Jenna?"

"I was scared," she confessed, "but then I just told myself to calm down. I kept telling myself everything will be all right because I am with my dad."

Some of the spiritual ledges you'll see in the coming pages have the potential to strike real fear into you. But there is no fear in risking spiritually and trusting God, who is bigger than your fear of stepping off. Your Father is with you to take you safely off the ledge into the unknown waters of His will and escort you safely to the next jumping-off point. In the chapters that follow you will learn how to safely jump into the risky waters of:

- fierce loyalty
- singular obedience to God's Word
- abandoning approval
- dangerous service
- killing sin
- aggressive honesty
- man-zone responsibility
- freedom through authentic friendships

- imitating Christ
- speaking boldly in the moment
- changing another's life
- accepting pain
- powerfully masculine emotions

You will be reading many stories about God's men—ones who stepped out in faith and others who shrank back in fear. You will see how a life of risking for God leads to freedom and how risking less leads to bondage. You'll definitely laugh. You might cry. You might fall to your knees in the middle of a chapter. Whatever you might feel or be motivated to do as a result of this journey toward courageous faith—listen to God and know that many of your brothers around the world are fighting this same battle to trust God in bigger ways.

Ready to jump? Then take your Father's hand, thank God for that feeling in the pit of your stomach, start turning these pages, and start living the way you were created to live—daring greatly for God.

chapter 2

mach 1 loyalty

We ought to abhor the thought of obtaining honor
by compromising our faith.

—CHARLES SPURGEON

In 1945 Chuck Yeager was an assistant maintenance officer in the fighter test section at Wright Field in Dayton, Ohio. He loved everything about his job except his prospects for advancement. He had the passion, skills, and knowledge to be a test pilot but not the education. So he fixed and flew planes thinking to himself that at least he was guaranteed time in the cockpit. The most exciting days were when the new planes landed in his shop, especially the jet aircraft in development. In *his* mind, he was so close and yet so far from his dream.

Flight Test Commander Colonel Albert Boyd had a dream too—to take the best pilot supersonic. The good news was that planes were in development and headed his way. The bad news was that the colonel was unsettled about finding a man in his pilot corps who could match these complex aircraft with equal knowledge of them and translate that knowledge directly into the cockpit *during flight.*

In the fall of 1945 the Lockheed P-80 Shooting Star—America's first operational jet fighter—was slated to be tested in the Mojave Desert. Boyd's team of test pilots packed their bags, fell in, and began boarding a bus that would take them to Muroc Air Base in California when they noticed a new face making his way aboard with Colonel Boyd.

Flying planes was as natural as breathing, but as smart as Yeager was, this part of school was a battle.

The looks on their faces all said, "Is that the maintenance officer?"

It seems that Yeager had been on Boyd's radar the entire time he was at Wright Field and that his flying ability and knowledge of mechanical systems had not gone unnoticed. The colonel had been secretly matrixing his own strict standards and passion for the project with the characters of the men under his command. On that basis Yeager was extended an invitation. To encourage him further, the colonel selected Captain Yeager to personally ferry one of the new P-80 fighters back to Wright Field (a.k.a. a private joy ride).

How quickly things had changed. Just a week earlier he was a maintenance officer with a dying dream. But now, as he blazed through the skies of North America, he was on his way to becoming a test pilot.

Test pilot school was not easy. The aeronautics, physics, and mathematics of jet flight were going to be critical for Yeager should he be the one to take jet aircraft supersonic. Flying planes was as natural as breathing, but as smart as Yeager was, this part of school was a battle.

Then, seemingly out of nowhere, Yeager hooked up with a flight engineer named Jack Ridley, whose gift was explaining complex math and physics. For both Ridley and Yeager it seemed destiny had delivered the right man at the right time. In the coming weeks and months this partnership would prove mission critical.

The buzz about Bell Aircraft's experimental new jet hit Colonel Boyd's ears like a mortar round. They were building it specifically to exceed the speed of sound and called it the X-1. It was a tiny plane with titanic capability and many new twists:

- The design was fashioned after a .50 caliber bullet since bullets traveled faster than the speed of sound.
- The power was supplied by four rocket engines.
- To prevent structural disintegration, it was made to withstand eighteen times the force of gravity.
- The X-1 would not take off from the ground; it would be carried aloft by a B-29 Superfortress, be dropped free, and then it would fire its engines.
- The pilot would have a grand total of three minutes of fuel to achieve supersonic speed before gliding back to earth.

Ironically, Boyd caught wind of Bell's X-1 project because of a public financial squabble with their pilot! So he seized the moment and successfully lobbied to have the whole program moved over to his command. The only remaining question was: Who would be the lucky cowboy to ride this aircraft into history? *Wanted: an experienced pilot with coconuts that won't crack under pressure.*

An open call to apply for the test pilot position was announced. It had to be voluntary because it was well known that other men had made attempts at supersonic but paid for it with their lives. Yeager applied, but self-doubt over his book smarts still lingered. Once again Colonel Boyd did not share that doubt. Instead he felt that Yeager's motivation, passion for his aircraft, raw flying ability, and ability to stay focused under pressure were the intangibles that, when added together, made the decision an easy one. To all the other pilots' disappointment, Chuck Yeager was chosen (along with his friend Ridley as the flight engineer), and the mission took shape.

Instead he felt that Yeager's motivation, passion for his aircraft, raw flying ability, and ability to stay focused under pressure were the intangibles that, when added together, made the decision an easy one.

In August 1947 eight powered flights were made, each providing new data and new obstacles. Hurdles included:

- Major turbulence: the closer to mach speed, the worse the turbulence became.
- Shock waves: disruptions on the plane's control surfaces made operating the plane impossible at .94 mach. Controls suddenly ceased to function on the seventh flight, requiring Yeager to kill power, jettison fuel, and glide back down.

- Nose instability: the ability to operate the elevator that controlled the pitch of the nose was lost approaching mach speed, influencing the angle of attack and preventing greater speed.

Prior to the eighth flight, Ridley theorized that they could control the plane near mach speeds using the horizontal stabilizer instead of the elevator to correct their angle of attack. On the eighth flight Yeager tested the concept at mach .96, and his buddy was right. Buoyed by the developments, Colonel Boyd decided they would take the X-1 to mach .98 on the next run. Prospects for supersonic were on the horizon until turbulence of another kind jeopardized the next flight.

On October 12 (two days before the next flight) Yeager and his wife were riding horses. To finish the ride they decided to race the horses back to the barn, thinking a gate to the barn was open. Instead, the gate was bolted shut! Yeager's horse hit the gate almost at full speed, and Yeager was launched unwillingly into near-supersonic flight. The result was two broken ribs just two days before the big day.

This presented unique problems for Captain Yeager. For starters, an X-1 pilot did not enter the cockpit like a traditional fighter jet. He had to enter through a tiny side door. Easy enough. But once inside, he had to pull the door into place. *Ouch!* Then the door had to be latched from the inside by pushing a lever forward to lock the cockpit door. *Triple-dog ouch!* He simply couldn't do it. He confessed his secret to Ridley, and as they mulled over the dilemma, Ridley had an engineer's epiphany. Never at a loss at solving complex problems, Ridley fashioned a makeshift handle out of a broomstick. Yeager could use the stick to pull the door closed, push the lever, and lock the cockpit door. Meanwhile, Colonel Boyd remained blissfully in the dark.

On the morning of October 14, 1947, Yeager and his broomstick entered the cockpit of the X-1 and lifted off in the B-29 making its way to target altitude for the ninth time. Myriad questions coursed through everyone's minds as the signal arrived from the B-29 pilot that target altitude had been achieved.

Poof! The X-1 sliced through the supersonic barrier on a sheet of glass.

Three. Two. One.

Upon separation, Yeager immediately fired the X-1's rocket engines and, in a matter of seconds, rapidly approached a previously unknown realm.

At .94 mach the plane began to rattle. He engaged the horizontal stabilizer trim switch instead of the elevator *(thank you, Ridley),* ignited the fourth engine, and watched the mach meter as the needle jumped forward off the scale.

Poof! The X-1 sliced through the supersonic barrier on a sheet of glass. Ground operators mistook the historic sonic boom for thunder crashing in the distance. Back in the cockpit, Chuck Yeager decided to fly in his newly discovered realm of supersonic flight for twenty glorious seconds before turning off two engines and decelerating back to subsonic speeds.

An invisible barrier was no more. "A poke through Jell-O" was how Yeager described the historic event.

The Loyalty Barrier

As I work with men all over the world, they tell me about their battles to break through the inner spiritual barrier of total loyalty to Jesus Christ.

Whether it's soldiers e-mailing me from Iraq or guys in my own congregation, they all lament disloyalty to their King and are frustrated by their lapses in spiritual loyalty. It eats at them that they cannot seem to break through and enter that new realm of spiritual life and loyalty that noble men of God possess in abundance.

They are not alone. I believe that millions are coming up short and settling for subsonic existences believing the lie that only "special" men can be loyal to God in all they do. The gaps in their lives lead many men to make the fatal mistake of lowering the bar of God's Word so as not to be on the hook for strong passages such as, "Just as he who called you is holy, so be holy in all you do" (1 Peter 1:15). In our shame, we desensitize our spirits to His voice, become critical of others who are succeeding, and, in the process, achieve new spiritual lows. Gary speaks for all of us when he writes:

> Kenny,
>
> The problem is this: lately it feels like everything is falling apart. I am struggling with work and with my family. I have not fully surrendered to God and am still living loyally to myself in many ways. I do not want this anymore. I want to be the man God has designed me to be. I have come to the realization that I need to be 100 percent loyal to God, not 80/20 as I have been. Dude, I do not know what to do next. How can I make the transition to the next level?
>
> Gary

All God's men are called to break through the spiritual loyalty barrier and move from a fragile and fickle heart commitment to a fierce loyalty in Christ. Sure, it's a process and, more important, a fight. But like reaching mach 1, once you have tasted the power, adventure, and freedom of this new realm, your taste for subsonic commitment changes dramatically.

In "man-world," loyalty is a big deal. In fact, it is a man's most meaningful expression of love to another man. Look at our friendships. To us the language of loyalty and the language of love diffuse effortlessly into each other. If we love someone, we are loyal to that person. So when the Bible calls on us to risk loving God with all our heart, soul, mind, and strength, the masculine mind-set feels a stronger call to allegiance over *amore,* if you catch my drift. Wherever you find a strong allegiance in a man, you will find a strong affection, and vice versa. Think Jonathan and David, or a Boston Red Sox fan. Either one makes my point.

I believe that millions are coming up short and settling for subsonic existences believing the lie that only "special" men can be loyal to God in all they do.

But a lot of our loyalty is royally misplaced. Thousands of e-mails tell me that we prefer other commitments:

- cyber-tingles below the belt over total commitment to our wives
- evading spiritual conversations over engaging in them
- keeping up spiritual images over cultivating spiritual substance
- winning arguments over winning healthy relationships
- incoming cash over "kingdom come"
- missionary positions over loyalty to God's mission
- self-service over serving others

The reason we get our priorities confused is because, at the root of it all, our loyalty to Jesus Christ is diluted. It's not hard to see, either. Loyalties drive our priorities. Our priorities drive our choices. The actions that follow reinforce either health or harm in our relationships with others and with God.

Marriage is a prime example. I can *say* I am loyal to my wife, Chrissy. I can stand at the altar and make a vow to be loyal forever. But this does not mean I have a strong relationship, healthy intimacy, or good priorities. All it says is that I have given a sign of my intention to be loyal. True loyalty comes through what I *do*—specific actions that are meaningful to Chrissy. Those will tell the real story.

This connection between our allegiances and our actions was not lost on Jesus as it related to His men. He pushed mach 1 allegiance because He knew the stakes were high for every one of His men and every life they would touch for His kingdom. Reconsider this sonic boom conversation with Peter:

> Jesus: "Simon son of John, do you *truly* love me more than these?"
> Peter: "Yes, Lord, you know that I love you."
> Jesus: "Feed my lambs."
> Jesus again: "Simon son of John, do you *truly* love me?"
> Peter: "Yes, Lord, you know that I love you."
> Jesus: "Take care of my sheep."
> Jesus again: "Simon son of John, do you love me?"
> Peter: "Lord, you know all things; you know that I love you."
> Jesus: "Feed my sheep. I tell you the truth, when you were younger you dressed yourself and went where you wanted; but

> when you are old you will stretch out your hands, and someone else will dress you and lead you where you do not want to go." Jesus said this to indicate the kind of death by which Peter would glorify God.
>
> Jesus again: "Follow me!" (see John 21:15–19, emphasis added)

Jesus doesn't give up on us when we are disloyal, but make no mistake—He likes His men uber-loyal. I would not want to have been Peter in this conversation, having my loyalty questioned. At the same time, I love the fact that Jesus demanded loyalty before reinstating Peter to the team. Peter was God's man being prepared to do God's work in his generation. To this end, Jesus knew that Peter's personal loyalty and love for Him had to break the normal boundaries if he was to fulfill God's purpose for his life. Ordinary loyalty does not produce extraordinary anything.

Jesus doesn't give up on us when we are disloyal, but make no mistake—He likes His men uber-loyal.

Fast forward to Acts chapter three. The same guy who said, "I don't know him" and "What are you talking about?" has found a spine. What a contrast! Listen to his words here as the mach needle goes off the chart. Peter stands in front of the same men who mutilated his Messiah and declares:

> The God of Abraham, Isaac and Jacob, the God of our fathers, has glorified his servant Jesus. You handed him over to be killed, and you disowned him before Pilate, though he had decided to let him go. You disowned the Holy and Righteous One and asked that a murderer be released to you. You killed the author of life, but God raised him from the dead. We are witnesses of this.... Repent, then,

> and turn to God, so that your sins may be wiped out, that times of refreshing may come from the Lord, and that he may send the Christ, who has been appointed for you—even Jesus." (Acts 3:13–15, 19–20)

Peter goes public with his faith and shatters the loyalty barrier.

Follow his progression. *You disowned him. You let him go. You made an unholy exchange of good for bad. Come back! Experience forgiveness and renewal.* Anything about this conversation sound familiar? Firm confrontation? A strong call? Forgiveness and reconnection to God's team? Peter experienced this same process with Jesus. And just as Jesus did with him, Peter firmly confronts the men of Jerusalem, offers them a clear path back to Christ, and promises them a refreshing renewal in their relationship with God. The Christ-rejecter leads the Christ-killers back to Christ! No man is *ever* out of the game for good.

After the resurrection it appears Peter still counted himself out of the game. He went back to fishing. But just as Colonel Boyd saw the potential in Chuck Yeager, Jesus wanted to use Peter's passion and skills to build the kingdom. That's exactly why Jesus cared enough about Peter to push him hard on the loyalty question. He knew that the pain of betrayal could be used to create a loyalty and a bond so strong that He would never have to ask again. In fact, Peter's taste for compromise was *never* the same again, and ultimately, his loyalty extended to his own crucifixion.

God's man can be transformed from unbelievable disloyalty to supersonic allegiance if he's willing to be examined honestly by God.

Spiritual Sonic Booms

If you watch film of a modern fighter aircraft on the verge of mach 1, you see a kind of halo appear around the aircraft. It's both mysteriously odd and beautiful. The halo encapsulates the pilot and plane, signaling a transition from subsonic to supersonic, from resistance to release. This phenomenon parallels our spiritual breakthroughs of the heart. We have moments of transition, of progress, and of growth where God's Holy Spirit encapsulates our commitment to Christ and raises it to new levels. But we must persevere in pursuit of Christ, withstand failures, try again, and rally others to help us get in position to make that transition. Major breakthroughs require dogged determination.

Chuck Yeager's journey is a lot like our own, peppered with passion for God mixed with doubts about ourselves, turbulent spiritual forces, and unforeseen obstacles.

In our quest to experience the power and freedom that total loyalty to Jesus provides God's man, we are bound to encounter problems, obstacles, challenges, and doubts about ever being free of our sinful and dark desires. Chuck Yeager's journey is a lot like our own, peppered with passion for God mixed with doubts about ourselves, turbulent spiritual forces, and unforeseen obstacles. And yet our allegiance to the cross of Christ and our desire to honor that drives us forward and keeps us risking again and again for Jesus in the face of a determined opposition.

The turbulence we feel over temptations to compromise comes from the real presence of the Disloyal One. His agents court our character flaws and magnify our fears to keep us subsonic and bound to inaction. A true God's man understands these dynamics and expects increased buffeting and shock waves coming against him. He knows these invisible forces are spiritual attempts to disrupt his angle of approach toward new levels of confidence in God and commitment to God. The Enemy knows we are on the verge of creating historic moments in our spiritual journeys and reaching a point of no return.

Writing this book is a perfect example. My commitment was made long ago to write a book on risking it all to be God's man. When the time came to start writing it, I began having horrible dreams, sensing the presence of the Evil One. Unusual circumstances at work and at home rose up to interrupt the writing schedule. Bizarre interpersonal conflicts came into my life, which temporarily but totally caught me off guard. At times just the fatigue brought on by juggling marriage, family, pastoring, Every Man Ministries, mission trips, traveling, and speaking taxed my mind and body so hard that I had trouble sleeping. The ironic thing is that this happens prior to and at the outset of *every* book I write. Why the huge resistance? Because it represents my commitment to being loyal to Christ in using my gifts for Him, and it also represents the strengthening of millions of lives. Satan fears any man who exchanges fear and a safe life for mach 1 loyalty and commitment. I knew better than to go into this project without the "stabilizing force" of a well-oiled team of prayer warriors. But with some Holy Spirit engineering, that deficit was corrected, and you are holding the result in your hands.

It takes perseverance to get into halo position and an awareness of the turbulence that always precedes the moment of breakthrough.

As turbulent as your commitment to Christ might be, recognize those shock waves as an indication that you're on the verge of a new spiritual plateau. Progress may seem slow, but with God's help and power, as well as some committed spiritual Ridleys in your life, you keep getting into that cockpit, lifting off, and surging ahead. You zero in on the obstacles and discover God's solutions, realizing that the more turbulence you sense, the closer you are to the next spiritual breakthrough. You persevere with eager expectation, and when the time comes, you will fire that fourth rocket and successfully obliterate the barriers of fear and lack of trust by the power of courageous commitment. When this happens, God's man booms with thunderous energy. These are the sonic booms of spiritual freedom:

- Boom! *I please God over man every time.*
- Boom! *I am loyal to God's purposes over my own.*
- Boom! *I do not blend with my culture; I battle because I am loyal to the blood.*
- Boom! *I am never embarrassed to be called a Christian—I wear my identity like a Marine. Semper Fi!*
- Boom! *I do not shrink back from spiritual conversations.*
- Boom! *I am disloyal to the "old" voice pattern of sin.*
- Boom! *I am loyal to the Holy Spirit in me, calling me to live right.*
- Boom! *I am loyal to my God-given mission in the world.*

Loyalty to God is not created in a vacuum. It is forged and formed in our hearts through situations that call for it. Those situations are critical to getting you into position along your spiritual journey. That is why the Scriptures encourage us to hang on to our allegiance to Jesus like a pilot going after a speed record. "Don't lose your grip on Love and Loyalty. Tie them around your neck; carve their initials on your heart" (Proverbs 3:3,

MSG). In other words, it takes perseverance to get into halo position and an awareness of the turbulence that always precedes the moment of breakthrough.

Want to flick the switch on that fourth engine? Are you ready for your halo moment? Risk loyalty.

Lord Jesus,

By Your power, I invite kingdom loyalty to come and rule over my heart. Strengthen my grip on Your love for me, and tattoo Your initials on my heart.

Amen.

chapter 3

one man's obedience

Beware of the inclination to dictate to God as to what you will allow to happen if you obey him.

—Oswald Chambers

Chiune Sugihara was a good Japanese son. His family had the good rural samurai values one might expect: family, responsibility, and honor. That's why Chiune's father was so incredulous when, upon graduating from high school, Chiune announced he was *not* going to study to become a doctor. Instead, the young son had decided to go to work in Tokyo as a part-time longshoreman and tutor to finance his education in English at a prestigious university.

The Japanese equivalent of "You *what?!*" is said to have been heard echoing from Yokuska to Tokyo. His dream was not his father's dream. Chiune wanted to study literature and live far away from his native soil. A young man with an eye on the horizon and a mind for learning, his will to adventure could not be tamed.

It wasn't long before Chiune came across a classified ad to study abroad. It was perfect:

> JAPANESE FOREIGN MINISTRY SEEKS APPLICANTS WHO WISH TO STUDY ABROAD WITH INTEREST IN FOREIGN SERVICE. MUST TAKE ENTRANCE EXAM TO QUALIFY.

After acing the entrance exam, young Chiune found himself at the Japanese Language Institute in Harbin, China. He added Russian to his English studies and graduated with honors in time to serve his country following the Japanese expansion into Manchuria. The real shocker for his family was not Chiune's exodus out of Japan but his conversion to Christianity in China. A professional journey morphed into a spiritual discovery that would change the course of his life and the legacy he would leave.

The real shocker for his family was not Chiune's exodus out of Japan but his conversion to Christianity in China.

Chiune Sugihara did not waste any time getting on the fast track. In Japanese-controlled Manchuria he served in the Foreign Affairs Department, quickly advancing to vice minister at the ripe old age of thirty. After negotiating the purchase of the Russian-owned Manchurian railroad system for his government—infuriating the Russians and saving the Japanese government a fortune—things seemed to be lining up. He was on deck for the minister of foreign affairs post in Manchuria when his government's politics began conflicting with his identity as God's man for the first but not the last time. If intimidation and cruelty were part of the job description, Chiune's personal convictions would not allow him to accommodate or participate. Instead of passively acquiescing and being a "team player," he protested the injustices, eventually resigning his post in 1934. Chiune Sugihara's fast track had turned into gridlock.

Four years later, Chiune was in the game once again. Called back by his government, this time he landed in Helsinki, Finland, but was quickly moved to Lithuania to open a one-man consulate in 1939. War developments required a Japanese presence close to the action. With the Soviet Union to the east and Nazi Germany to the west, Lithuania became an intelligence station for the Japanese. It was a powder-keg assignment, and the fuse was going to be short.

After Hitler's invasion of Poland in the fall of 1939, intelligence started coming in through Jewish refugees fleeing Poland. The news was unfathomable: tens of thousands of Jews were being murdered by the Nazis. The city in which Chiune's consulate was located was also home to more than thirty thousand Lithuanian Jews, most of whom did not believe the stories and denied the same thing could ever happen there. But in the summer of 1940, reality struck, and the Soviet Union bullied, invaded, and forcibly occupied Lithuania. No Jews could leave except the Polish refugees, and *only if* they obtained the right travel documents. Lithuania became a prison, the rest of Europe barring the emigration of refugees from any Nazi-occupied territory. Morbid fear slowly began to replace hope for the Lithuanian Jews.

In July 1940, as Hitler's armies advanced eastward, Soviet authorities instructed all foreign embassies to leave Lithuania. All but two complied: the Dutch and Chiune Sugihara. Sugihara asked for and, surprisingly, received a twenty-day extension.

With the clock ticking, the Polish Jews came up with a last-ditch plan that hinged on the Japanese consul's granting transit visas. The documents, combined with those from the Dutch and Soviet consuls, would ensure Jewish refugees could safely land on two Dutch islands in the Caribbean. The Dutch and Soviet consuls assured cooperation, and Japan became the passageway from death to life.

In late July, Chiune Sugihara looked out his window at the consulate to see hundreds of Jewish families forming a line around the grounds. After learning about the path to freedom the refugees hoped to follow, Sugihara was deflated. He did not have the authority to grant Japanese transit visas. That would have to come direct from Tokyo, and he already knew how that request would be received. Yet hoping against hope, he wired the foreign ministry in Japan three times for permission to issue visas to Jewish refugees. Three separate requests were flatly denied. His repeated attempts angered the brass in Tokyo, and they moved to quash all hope by wiring a final communication to Sugihara:

He wired the foreign ministry in Japan three times for permission to issue visas to Jewish refugees. Three separate requests were flatly denied.

> CONCERNING TRANSIT VISAS REQUESTED PREVIOUSLY STOP ADVISE ABSOLUTELY NOT TO BE ISSUED TO ANY TRAVELER NOT HOLDING A FIRM END VISA WITH GUARANTEED DEPARTURE EXIT JAPAN STOP NO EXCEPTIONS STOP NO FURTHER INQUIRIES EXPECTED STOP
>
> SIGNED, K TANAKA FOREIGN MINISTRY TOKYO

For the man raised on samurai values, the chain of command had spoken. He had the transit visas but not the permission. For another man, that might have settled it. But there was another chain of command at play the foreign ministry hadn't considered—the highest one.

After receiving this last cable, Sugihara gathered together his family to tell them the news and what had to be done. For the next twenty-nine days, Chiune Sugihara and his wife handwrote transit visas day and night. Three hundred visas a day were written and given to Jews fleeing the coming Holocaust. Chiune worked unceasingly, not even stopping to eat, afraid of losing any time. His wife fed him while he wrote, massaging his aching hands so that he could keep writing. Crowds of hundreds became throngs of thousands as the race against time and closure of the consulate drew near. He wrote and wrote and wrote, even passing a few more precious visas through his train window as he was leaving for Berlin.

As the train pulled out, he finally handed the coveted consul stamp to a refugee who, in turn, used it to save many more Jews from Hitler's death camps. Sugihara's only regret was that he could not do more.

By war's end, Chiune Sugihara's visas had saved the lives of more than six thousand Jews. After the war, the Japanese government dismissed Sugihara from diplomatic service—the fate he expected. Instead of signing treaties or hosting dignitaries abroad, he would live out the remainder of his days selling light bulbs in Japan.

Now some sixty-five years later, estimates are that more than forty thousand people are alive today because of Chiune Sugihara. They are known as "Sugihara's Survivors." In 1986, one year before his death, Sugihara was asked why he did it. He answered, "I may have to disobey my government, but if I don't, I would be disobeying God." When his story became public near the end of his life, his son was asked, "How did your father feel about his choice?" The young son replied, "My father's life was fulfilled. When God needed him to do the right thing, he was available to do it." Sugihara was given Israel's highest honor by the Holocaust Memorial and declared Righteous Among the Nations for his self-sacrifice.

In other words, Sugihara was God's man.

Chain Reactions

One man's obedience brings life to many. We simply do not know how far-reaching one act of obedience to God will be and what consequences our choice will have for others. This reason alone would be enough to seek God's will in all matters. When the moment of our greatest challenge arrives, we want to be in the habit of saying yes to God rather than debating or compromising. Being ready means we aren't considering our own rewards or consequences, but the impact of our choices upon others. This is the kind of unselfish obedience that is most like Jesus Christ's. While there may be some wrestling, we want to have a strong spiritual resolve to see God's will done.

When the moment of our greatest challenge arrives, we want to be in the habit of saying yes.

Spiritual obedience and spiritual disobedience set in motion consequences we cannot undo. *All* decisions that affect our relationships with God and others involve defying one voice and obeying another. Sugihara's choice to obey God meant simultaneously that he would defy "K TANAKA" from the foreign ministry. The moment he made up his mind for God, he set in motion a chain reaction that extends physically and spiritually into eternity. Sugihara's story serves as a parable of how God wants all His men to live. Why? Because just as the future of thousands of Jews hinged on one man's actions, all of human history hinged on the choices of two men to obey or not to obey God.

> Just as the result of one trespass was condemnation for all men, so also the result of one act of righteousness was justification that brings life for all men. For just as through the disobedience of the one man the many were made sinners, so also through the obedience of the one man the many will be made righteous." (Romans 5:18–19)

Two men. Two different choices. Two different chain reactions.

	ADAM	JESUS
Act	disobedience	obedience
Nature of Act	trespassing	sacrificing
Impact Zone	all men	all men
Consequence	sin to men	grace to men
Judgment	condemnation	salvation
Result	death	eternal life
Future	separation from God	eternal union with God

What chain reactions is your obedience or disobedience creating in eternity? It's a sobering thought if you're like me and have a colorful past. When we realize the progression of the disobedience of Adam, we can start to understand the passion of Jesus on this whole issue of doing life God's way. It makes more sense to believe that Jesus was big on obedience with His men *not* because He wanted strict, legalistic adherence to the guidelines, but because He was aiming to correct the chain reaction: the destruction of disobedience by God's first man. I think we would have some of this same energy if correcting another man's mistake meant crucifixion for us. We should thank Him for telling us:

- "Whoever has my commands *and obeys them,* he is the one who loves me. He who loves me will be loved by my Father, and I too will love him and show myself to him" (John 14:21, emphasis added).

  Reminder: closeness to God is a function of faith expressed through loving obedience to His commands. You are as close to God as you choose to be.
- "Now that you know these things, you will be blessed if you do them" (John 13:17).

  Reminder: we're accountable for what we know, and we live large as God's men when we act on it.
- "Anyone who breaks one of the least of these commandments and teaches others to do the same will be called least in the kingdom of heaven, but whoever practices and teaches these commands will be called great in the kingdom of heaven" (Matthew 5:19).

  Reminder: rationalizing the commands away doesn't let you off the hook.

When I was a student at UCLA, my friends and I would talk with other students about knowing God, using a great little booklet called the *Four Spiritual Laws.* My favorite page in the booklet had these two circles on it. Each circle potentially represented your life. Each circle had a seat in it representing control. In one circle there was no one on the seat, and in the other there was a cross on the seat, representing Christ in the life and in control. Right below the diagram there were two questions:

- "Which circle best represents your life?"
- "Which circle would you like to have represent your life?"

It was always a rush when someone would realize the chaos of life without Christ and come to that moment of decision that would change their eternal future.

Look back at the chain reaction chart and ask yourself:

- *Which column best represents my life right now?*
- *Which column would I like to represent my life going forward?*

It doesn't matter if you're a pastor of a thirty-thousand-member church or a brand-new believer. The questions for God's men are always: *Am I going to do life my way or God's way? What does God require of me in this situation? What is God telling me? What does His Word say? What will honor Him most? Am I going to trust God's promise or try to make it happen on my own?*

Some of you reading this are saying to yourselves, "Yeah, yeah, Kenny. I know this already. Where's the meat?" Trust me, brother, your faith in God's character, His Word, and your deep-down conviction of who He wants you to be and what He wants you to do is the twenty-ounce prime-cut steak of Christianity. When you go to Outback Steakhouse, you can order the coconut shrimp or a salad. But is that why a *man* goes to Outback Steakhouse? A seasoned, seared steak is why I go. That's their signature. That's what a steakhouse is known for, and that's why I put my name in, wait for a table, and lay down an Andrew Jackson when I'm done. Nothing against the veggies, but it's definitely the beef that makes me a repeat customer.

If God's Man is your identity—your "signature," to borrow from our Outback Steakhouse analogy—then the main characteristic your spiritual life hangs on is one thing: faith expressed through obedience. This was the test for Adam in the garden. This was the issue when God told Noah to build the boat. This was the gauntlet for Abraham when God asked him to leave home and "go to the land I will show you" with no clue where that was (Genesis 12:1). It was the issue with Moses bringing Pharaoh a message from his Maker. Obedience was the issue when Joshua and God's people crossed the Jordan River. Not taking God at His Word was King Saul's flaw, but taking God at His Word was King David's strength (mostly). The legacies of the kings in the Old Testament are based on whether they did evil or good "in the eyes of the LORD" during their reigns (2 Kings 21:2). You get the picture: you can look like a duck, but if you don't waddle and quack, you are a decoy.

You get the picture: you can look like a duck, but if you don't waddle and quack, you are a decoy.

Actually, I often need this reminder myself: I know way more than I obey. I'm far more educated in what I need to be thinking and doing than I actually pull off in my real-time, day-to-day choices. So the goal of every God's man, including me, is to close that gap as best he can. King David in the Bible got pretty far on this one when other men fell short (King Saul in this case). God described him this way:

> After Saul had ruled forty years, God removed him from office and put King David in his place, with this commendation: "I've searched the land and found this David, son of Jesse. *He's a man whose heart beats to my heart, a man who will do what I tell him.*" (Acts 13:21–22, MSG, emphasis added)

What does God like to see most in us when He speaks into our lives? Inner agreement matched by prompt obedience. If we're known for anything, it should be for our willingness to respond to God's direction in the face of great personal risk. It's easy to obey in our pleasures, but it's not so easy in our pains. The real measure of God's men is our willingness to do what God tells us to do, even when it means losing:

What does God like to see most in us when He speaks into our lives? Inner agreement matched by prompt obedience.

- money
- a relationship
- a good feeling
- a secret
- a job opportunity
- our image at church
- friends
- possessions
- a dream
- control over the outcome

Loss for the sake of loss is stupidity. But suffering a loss, real or imagined, for obedience to Christ is faith at its very best. The reason God loves prompt obedience is that it exposes the authentic God's man from the synthetic poser.

> We know that we have come to know [the Lord] if we obey his commands. The man who says, "I know him," but does not do what he commands is a liar, and the truth is not in him. But if

> anyone obeys his word, God's love is truly made complete in him. (1 John 2:3–5)

Heavy words. When we risk for obedience, the message we send is clear:

- God means what He says.
- God does what He says.
- God is able to accomplish whatever He commits to doing.

Grateful Obedience

The guys at Saddleback Church are used to hearing me say, "If you don't have an attitude of gratitude, all you have left is *attitude.*" In other words, if I am not grateful to God for His many blessings and for His grace expressed to me in Christ, the only other options are to act like (a) I deserve them or (b) I have earned them myself. Both of these mind-sets are symptoms of pride. Why press the issue? Because I know that if a man gets this right, he will make outstanding spiritual progress. *Fact time:* gratitude is the Roto-Tiller of the heart; it softens up the soil both to receive and to act upon the Word of God.

That's why I love communion at our men's gatherings. It's like a gratitude machine with me and our men. We get to sit at the foot of the cross for a good while and take a long hard look at true commitment, obedience, and love in the body of Jesus. We remember that He gave His today for our tomorrows. And when we look with eyes open, His love pours into our hearts and does not let go.

Through communion, I connect with Jesus as a man, emotionally and relationally rather than intellectually. For when any man gets in touch with grace (when I get what I don't deserve) and mercy (when I don't get what I do deserve) and how God has graciously showered us with both by means of a bloody Savior, it's powerful. Those courageous enough to open their hearts to this kind of grace and mercy repent from all self-sufficiency and renew their outlook on their lives for God. A new hunger is found to honor such love with faithful obedience.

It makes all the sense in the world that Jesus would not call us to faith and make obedience a burden. In fact, He chastised the toxic legalism of the Pharisees severely. Then He promised us He would show us love and commitment, and we, as His brothers, would respond with commitment of our own. "Greater love has no one than this, that he lay down his life for his friends. You are my friends if you do what I command" (John 15:13–14). See the connection? Jesus is saying there is no other thing He can do to motivate you to live life His way.

Obedience is the evidence that convinces the world that we are indeed grateful.

Obedience is the evidence that convinces the world that we are indeed grateful. What's pathetic is a man who has been the recipient of this grace and mercy but doesn't act like one. He's the type of guy who doesn't realize the price that was paid for his God-given life and is a candidate for God's discipline. Like a little boy, his attention wanders from the Word, and he is led away by his feelings or false pride. Sound familiar? Every dad knows this frustration with his own children, but many of us fail to see the correlation with our heavenly Father.

As any dad would feel, our grateful obedience brings joy to God. It is nothing short of a delight. We see this when Abraham completely trusted

God by obediently offering up Isaac, simply because it was God doing the asking. Let the cartwheels begin.

> "Do not lay a hand on the boy," [the angel of the LORD] said. "Do not do anything to him. Now I know that you fear God, because you have not withheld from me your son, your only son."
>
> Abraham looked up and there in the thicket he saw a ram caught by its horns. He went over and took the ram and sacrificed it as a burnt offering instead of his son. So Abraham called that place The LORD Will Provide. And to this day it is said, "On the mountain of the LORD it will be provided."
>
> The angel of the LORD called to Abraham from heaven a second time and said, "I swear by myself, declares the LORD, that because you have done this and have not withheld your son, your only son, I will surely bless you and make your descendants as numerous as the stars in the sky and as the sand on the seashore. Your descendants will take possession of the cities of their enemies, and through your offspring all nations on earth will be blessed, because you have obeyed me." (Genesis 22:12–18)

Dads delight in rewarding obedience. The way God responded here demonstrates a major spiritual principle, put well by scholar and pastor Stuart Briscoe. "The word heeded releases the power that's needed." I'll say! When Isaac asked Abraham, "Where is the lamb?" his dad replied, "God himself will provide the lamb" (Genesis 22:7–8).

The headline over Abraham's life as God's man could easily read: "I have considered my ways and have turned my steps to your statutes. I will hasten and not delay to obey your commands" (Psalm 119:59–60). Obedience preceded the release of God's power—a tangible expression of His delight at the trust Abraham displayed. I would not want to have been Abraham in that situation, but I am so glad he showed me how obedience really looks. As you can see, God got excited and received so much joy over Abraham's obedience that God blessed his legacy in ways Abraham would never fully comprehend in his own lifetime. His decision changed the earth!

So when you are tempted to think, *What difference does my obedience to God make?* remember the chain reactions God's men can start. You never know the full impact one act can have. God wants to release His power in ways you never dreamed, if you'll only believe that He means what He says. About everything.

chapter 4

liked or faithful?

We risk for him to the degree that we know we are loved by him.

—Brennan Manning

During the fourth great persecution (AD 162–180), cruelties against Christians were so horrific that onlookers were astonished that followers would not turn from Christ. As a committed Stoic philosopher, Emperor Marcus Aurelius had an ax to grind with Christians. His indifference to pain or pleasure was manifest in his energetic pursuit of believers in Jesus Christ. One man on the wanted list was a friend and disciple of the apostle John named Polycarp. His death and capture were recorded in history and are relayed in *The New Foxe's Book of Martyrs.*

> Polycarp, who was a student of the apostle John and the overseer of the church in Smyrna, heard that soldiers were looking for him and tried to escape but was discovered by a child. After feeding the guards who captured him, he asked for an hour in prayer, which they gave him. He prayed with such fervency, that his guards said

they were sorry that they were the ones who captured him. Nevertheless, he was taken to the governor and condemned to be burned in the market place.

After his sentence was given, the governor said to him, "Reproach Christ and I will release you."

Polycarp answered, "Eighty-six years I have served him, and he never once wronged me. How then shall I blaspheme my King who has saved me?"

In the market place, he was tied to the stake rather than nailed, as was the usual custom, because he assured them he would stand immovable in the flames and not fight them. As the dry sticks placed around him were lit, the flames rose up and circled his body without touching him. The executioner was then ordered to pierce him with a sword. When he did, a great quantity of blood gushed out and put out the fire. Although his Christian friends asked to be given his body as it was so they could bury him, the enemies of the Gospel insisted that it be burned in the fire, which was done.[1]

Has Christ ever once wronged you?

I shake when I read about God's men during the persecutions of Emperors Nero, Domitian, Trajan, and Hadrian and their willingness to risk their very breath in order to stand honorably for their Savior. More personally, I wonder what these God's men think of God's men in the new millennium. The writer of Hebrews tells us that their "witness" encapsulates our own: "Therefore, since we are surrounded by such a great cloud of witnesses, let us throw off everything that hinders and the sin that so easily entangles, and let us run with perseverance the race marked out for us" (Hebrews 12:1).

The Greek word translated "witnesses" is the root of the English word *martyr* and means "testifiers and witnesses." The testifiers are the people who bore testimony to the power of their faith and to God's faithfulness.

Push came to shove for Ignatius too. As the head pastor of the church in Antioch, he was recalled to Rome by Emperor Trajan because he unashamedly taught and professed Christ in Syria. While in Smyrna, he sent a communication ahead to the Roman Christians asking them to do something very unusual—don't intervene!

> Now I begin to be a disciple. I care for nothing of visible or invisible things so that I may but win Christ. Let fire and the cross, let the companies of wild beasts, let the breaking of the bones and the tearing of limbs, let the grinding of the whole body, and all the malice of the devil come upon me; be it so, only may I win Christ Jesus.

On the day of his execution, with the sounds of the roaring lions as the backdrop, his desire to suffer with Christ moved him to say, "I am the wheat of Christ; I am going to be ground with the teeth of wild beasts that I may be found pure bread."[2]

Where are the men like Polycarp and Ignatius today? Where could you find them? Where are God's men? the ones who know how to die well? the ones who willingly would give their last earthly measure of devotion not for the promise of a sexual orgy upon entrance into heaven but for the honor of sharing in the sufferings of Christ their King? Where are they?

"Be It So" Versus Being Liked

The Bible says that great expressions of faith and commitment are allowed so that you and I can feed off them spiritually and "throw off everything that hinders" *us* from standing for Christ (Hebrews 12:1). The statement that peels off and thunders strongly down the centuries is "Be it so."

This was Ignatius's constitution. The prospect of visible torture? Be it so. The invisible mental and emotional torture? Be it so. Death by fire? Be it so. Death by crucifixion? Be it so. Lion's jaws? Same. Broken and torn limbs? Yep. The worst the devil can dish out? Bring it on.

"Be it so" are the words of a man who has stopped caring about what men think—especially powerful men like the emperor Trajan. If Ignatius were living among us in the digital age, he would never, like many men today, tremble at the thought of disappointing people, bosses, friends, peers, neighbors, or the guy in seat 22A next to him. Instead of being incapable of direct and strong speech about his Savior, he would tell his story and leave the results in God's hands.

He would not hedge, waffle, or procrastinate in declaring his faith in order to play to people. He would not be scared silent by the simple threat of rejection. He wouldn't fear being abandoned, losing support, or not being able to cope with disapproval of his faith. "Be it so" are the words of a God's man whose personal commitments, actions, and words have zilch to do with living up to the expectations or standards of other people. Being faithful to Christ replaces being liked by people.

Finding "Be it so" air to breathe is really hard in today's world. Loss of a strong identity in Christ has created a culture of Christian men who are more at ease chasing cool and being liked. We want to be admired and respected but not really known. Sexual conquest, physical attractiveness, recognition, and status have landed many of God's men in a stupor of self-importance and spiritual insignificance.

It's a subtle game, but a game nonetheless. Instead of "Be it so," they are hitting off the crack pipe of being liked, which is too intoxicating to give up. Being liked by everyone is the wicked twin of "Be it so," a charade, an act, and a fraud. It's a shadow of what a real God's man is supposed to be. The only outcome of a life devoted to the shadow is a life controlled and dominated by sin because there is no honesty in that life. Because where there is no honesty, there is sickness of character which is expressed in sick conduct and sin. And we wonder why we fail in our relationships with God and people. In the end, neither buys our act.

What honored God during the Roman persecutions and still honors Him today is risking faithfulness in the face of rejection.

"Be it so" encourages God's man to throw off being liked forever. Ignatius would have loved the chorus to the worship anthem "Amazing Love" because the lyrics screamed his heart to honor Christ.

> Amazing love, I know it's true
> And it's my joy to honor you

What honored God during the Roman persecutions and still honors Him today is risking faithfulness in the face of rejection. Thousands of first- and second-century believers risked disapproval by men for approval by God.

They simply stopped caring about the consequences.

"I Don't Care"

A murdered wife. A one-armed man. An obsessed detective. The chase begins.

Maybe you saw the remake of the movie *The Fugitive* starring Harrison Ford as Dr. Richard Kimble and Tommy Lee Jones as U.S. Marshal Sam Gerard. It's an easy movie to like—innocent man gets the shaft in the courts and is wrongly convicted and sentenced to federal prison.

A miscarriage of justice foisted on a likable guy makes the victim the hero and the "good guys" the bad guys. The conscientious marshal played by Jones is a combination of Jeff Foxworthy and the Terminator. He's a smart redneck whose style is so focused and cocky it keeps everyone off balance and laughing. It's as if he has a sixth sense for getting into the heads of the convicts he's hunting. Unfortunately, the gift is real, and his team quickly converges on Kimble after temporarily losing him in the confusion of a train wreck.

The chase takes place in a labyrinth of water tunnels surrounding a large dam. Kimble makes one wrong turn, and suddenly, the hunter and the hunted are face to face, standing at the edge of the ginormous dam.

It's a desperate moment. You feel depressed thinking he's been captured way too quickly. *No! He can't get caught yet!* But it's already over. Kimble looks down at the water falling hundreds of yards to the base of the concrete wall. It would mean certain death jumping from such a height. The eyes of both men lock on each other, and Dr. Kimble finally speaks.

"I didn't kill my wife."

Yeah! That's right! He didn't! So what do you have to say to that Marshal Gerard?

The jaded lawman tilts his head and sardonically replies, "I don't care."

Faced with the realization, Kimble has no choice. He closes his eyes and jumps.

"I don't care" is a line famous in cinematic history. It is the ethos of Jones's character. Manically focused, comically skeptical, mocking and disdainful of a convicted murderer's expectation that his statement of innocence could sway him from hauling his butt back to prison. Empathy is *not* on the menu and certainly not on Tommy Lee Jones's face in the scene. No one has sympathy for a convicted murderer, least of all Gerard who has yet to discover Kimble is telling the truth.

We must stop wearing all the masks that get us "liked" by men at the expense of grieving the Holy Spirit.

"I don't care" is a ratified declaration of our God's-man constitution. We should have the same dogged cynicism, the same disdain, and the same offended sensibility when insecure voices within beg us to be a man pleaser over a God pleaser. There are some things we simply cannot afford to care about in light of our identity, our purpose, and our connection to Jesus Christ. We must stop wearing all the masks that get us "liked" by men at the expense of grieving the Holy Spirit.

Like Marshal Gerard, God's man is so caught up in his pursuit of God and putting the "fugitive" (the old you) where he belongs, second thoughts about currying compromise to win approval of men seems absurd. Rejection for the sake of Christ might bring a cynical laugh or two from those who don't know Him, but it also brings serious consequences. Whatever those might be, you will take the hit. Don't compromise for men, don't apologize, and don't shrink back.

> So do not throw away your confidence; it will be richly rewarded. You need to persevere so that when you have done the will of God, you will receive what he has promised. For in just a very little while,
>
> "He who is coming will come and will not delay.
> But my righteous one will live by faith.
> And if he shrinks back,
> I will not be pleased with him."
>
> But we are not of those who shrink back and are destroyed, but of those who believe and are saved. (Hebrews 10:35–39)

In the early church the only apostle to escape violent death was John. All the rest—James son of Zebedee, Philip, Matthew, James the half brother of Jesus, Matthias, Andrew, Mark, Peter, Paul, Jude, Bartholomew, Thomas, and Luke—all went to their brutal deaths willingly, passionately. Their courage bred more courage like a virus, and the Lord exploded the numbers of people being saved *in the midst of* being horribly disliked by the

Roman Empire. Every Christian living at that time lived daily with the possibility of being asked to bear witness to their faith. They didn't even have any legal rights!

John Piper comments that being a Christian during the waves of persecution was to risk your life. "The first three centuries of the Christian church set the pattern for growth under threat.... There's the risk. It was always there. Maybe we will be killed for being Christians. Maybe we won't. It is a risk. That was normal. And to become a Christian under those circumstances was right."[3]

The pattern of the early church is still the pattern we are to follow today. God's man risks being faithful to who he is because being somebody else is a lie and misses the mark of his high call—the call of Jesus to choose Him in front of men and be faithful to Him.

Deserter or Disciple?

Following Jesus Christ inevitably means coming to a crossroads about whom you will live to please. Our King did not take great pains to, shall we say, put His guys at ease before sending them out to represent Him. But He was honest about the cost and what He expected from them. There would be no 401(k), no health benefits, no salary, no company donkeys. Just repeated attempts at intimidation.

Would you have signed up for this?

> A student is not greater than the teacher. A servant is not greater than the master. The student shares the teacher's fate. The servant shares the master's fate. And since I, the master of the household,

> have been called the prince of demons, how much more will it happen to you, the members of the household! But don't be afraid of those who threaten you. For the time is coming when everything will be revealed; all that is secret will be made public. What I tell you now in the darkness, shout abroad when daybreak comes. What I whisper in your ears, shout from the housetops for all to hear!
>
> Don't be afraid of those who want to kill you. They can only kill your body; they cannot touch your soul. Fear only God, who can destroy both soul and body in hell....
>
> If anyone acknowledges me publicly here on earth, I will openly acknowledge that person before my Father in heaven. But if anyone denies me here on earth, I will deny that person before my Father in heaven. (Matthew 10:24–28, 32–33, NLT)

Any takers?

Not a lot of wiggle room there. Either you are a deserter or a disciple. There's no room for "deserples," men who wear their spiritual masks around and then side with the other guys when convenient. God's men have to kiss the middle ground good-bye. Jesus obliterated it from the radar. He had to because the middle ground would create all sorts of problems for His men in front of people. Specifically, the middle ground would engender:

- vacillation—fluctuating spiritual commitment
- hesitation—holding back in speaking the message
- intimidation—bulldozing the confidence of His guys
- rationalization—making it reasonable to cave in to public opinion

- paralyzation—making the disciples powerless and inactive
- trepidation—letting apprehension and panic rule their emotions about the mission

A commander briefing his troops before a combat mission doesn't say to his platoon, "Okay, men. This is gonna be a cakewalk. When we get up there, the enemy is going to be so amazed by us, they'll throw down their guns and ask how they can be like us. They're just gonna love you, and they'll probably even apologize for going to war in the first place. They'll all see our side, and, heck, by then it won't even matter if we all switch sides." Anybody listening to this would be in danger of going home in a body bag.

Either you are a deserter or a disciple. There's no room for "deserples."

On the contrary, Jesus says, "Men, they're gonna come at you with both barrels blazing. But we'll stand our ground. Don't you be intimidated. You've got a bigger gun. I'm your leader here, and these pipsqueaks who squawk and threaten you, they're yours. Unload on 'em—everything I've given you. If you'll stand with Me, you'll have nothing to fear."

In other words, "Choose Me over them, and I'll choose you for heaven." It's your choice.

Lives depend on the choices of God's men to be faithful. One man—Gene Ellerbee—is thankful for faithful men. He was an executive at Procter and Gamble who had never even heard the label "Christian businessman." If he had, he would have lumped them in with his wife—Christianity was for sissies and women. Ironically, his wife was praying and asking God for some of those "sissies" to get in the ring with her hubby.

The first sissy was a friend, former football player, and fighter pilot Gene had hooked up with in Breckenridge, Colorado, and hadn't seen in years. Gene was excited to catch up and relive some of the old times. They were both glad to see each other until the sissy spoke up while they were outside chopping wood.

"Something has happened in my life, Gene, that I would like to tell you about," his friend said. The sissy went on to boldly share his testimony about how he had given his life to Christ and the difference it was making. This tsunami sent Gene into a tailspin, making him very uncomfortable and eager for their weekend to come to an end.

The next sissy drove to Denver in his four-wheel-drive truck to visit because God had put Gene on his mind. "Gene," his friend began, "you need Christ in your life."

Hello! Gene thought. *What in the world is going on here? All my friends are turning into religious nutballs!*

The third sissy sat down next to him on the plane and, after introductions, explained he had just returned from Rome and a visit to the Vatican. Gene countered that he didn't have much interest in the pope and tried to squelch the conversation. The sissy didn't want to waste Gene's time discussing the pope either, as it turned out. Instead, the man simply said, "Either you accept Jesus Christ as your personal Savior, or you reject Him." When Gene got home that night, he talked with his wife about how to commit his life to Christ.

Three faithful men who made three runs at the hill of Gene Ellerbee's heart for Christ's sake. They weren't appreciated or liked. They were not well received. They created discomfort and friction. But they were faithful to live out what God was asking of them for the sake of their faith. I am sure that each man had his reservations, but each was compelled. Their King had never done them wrong, and in their hearts they said, "Be it so." They did not care about Gene Ellerbee's title or wealth or reservations. They did care about representing their Lord faithfully and did so independently of one another. Their combined commitment secured another man's salvation.

Jesus asked for a strong commitment to Him in front of men. He asked them to risk rejection from men for approval from God even when outnumbered and outgunned. A lot of men started strong when Jesus first began preaching and things were positive. But slowly and steadily the numbers dwindled to the point where the pressure to cave in and leave moved Jesus to ask a dangerous question.

> "You do not want to leave too, do you?" Jesus asked the Twelve.
>
> Simon Peter answered him, "Lord, to whom shall we go? You have the words of eternal life. We believe and know that you are the Holy One of God." (John 6:67–69)

Ah. Be it so, Lord Jesus.

chapter 5

you are the solution

On the plains of hesitation, bleach the bones of countless millions who, on the threshold of victory, sat down to wait, and in waiting, died.

—William Moulton Marston

Cocaine. Hangovers. Wanton sex. Addictive cycles. Add testosterone, a rough New Jersey upbringing, and athleticism. Bake at 350 degrees for several years. Mix 'em together and you get something that looks a lot like first-class hedonist Jim Muzikowski.

Jim works at a nightclub on the Columbia University campus where he's finishing up grad school (so add "smart" to the mix). God looks down from heaven and says, "Yep. Here's the man." But by Jim's own admission, the ingredients for God's greatest works often start where you least expect them.

The last year of grad school was a whirlwind. Three jobs, one full time with the New York City Fire Department, and one in a bar working nights. He doesn't look like a responsible guy to start up a kingdom work. I mean, shouldn't God be looking at a Christian college for a straight shooter, raised in the suburbs, and sexually pure? For what God wanted to do, the answer was an unequivocal, "No!"

So God decides to get this party started on a rugby field.

B. J. Warner is a minister at Lamb's Church in Times Square. He plays on the B team, Old Blue, the second best rugby club around. Jim plays on the A team but likes to watch the junior team grind one out for the club. On the sideline, Jim takes a snort of cocaine out of his Dixie cup, looks up, and sees a player from Old Blue take a blindside elbow in the chops. Though he doesn't know it, it's B.J., who then proceeds to get up, clock the guy, and provoke a bench-clearing brawl. When Jim finds out the guy who got ejected for throwing the roundhouse is the guy they call "the priest," he's drawn over to meet B.J. Embarrassed, but filled with God's Spirit, the rugby-playing, punch-throwing minister invites the coke-snorting grad student to church. God's man is faithful.

Shouldn't God be looking at a Christian college for a straight shooter, raised in the suburbs, and sexually pure? "No!"

Hookers and yuppies, street people in tatters, Wall Street suits, and many other Times Square flavors make Lamb's Church an amalgam of New York proportions. Two weeks later, to B.J.'s surprise, Muzikowski showed up at church. Even the sermon was engaging for a Jersey Catholic guy. But the real mind-blowing event was the chicken dinner.

Chicken dinner?

People chatting, laughing at jokes, enjoying their time together without artificial inducements. For Muzikowski, something isn't adding up. He looks at B.J. *Seems to have it together. He's just a real guy and likes rugby.* He can't explain it, so he comes back again the following week.

B.J. knows a seeker when he sees one. He's been praying for his new friend "Muz" ever since meeting him on the field. He's sure Lamb's Church is throwing Jim's whole world into a chaotic blender. Probably never saw a conflict before. He probably never even stopped to look. But the hangovers that lead to sleepovers that lead to takeover are obviously swamping Jim's soul and his ability to hold things together on his own.

Meanwhile, the pride that convinced Muz he could bootstrap these demons into submission by resolve and exercise isn't working. Every two weeks he recommits to sobriety, only to wane again. He quits the party life, fails, and despairs. Stops drinking, starts feeling good, and one drink with the boys lands him right back where he started. Relapse after relapse, it's as if he's playing catch-up with the people down at Lamb's Church who seem to have peace and a purpose he just can't seem to muster.

So how did they do it? he wonders. *Ask B.J.*

"Hey, Muz!" *Sounds genuinely glad for the call.* "Why don't you come to a Bible study with us Tuesday night?"

"Uh, well. Okay."

"Great! See ya there!"

Click.

"@#$%! What was I thinking?"

Jim shows up Tuesday night and meets a drug dealer, a former male prostitute, two New York Jets, and smiling B.J. Talk about a Bible study group! *And now they're talking about what? Taking a train to DC for a prayer breakfast with the president? Okay, this I gotta see.*

But wouldn't you know, Jim finds a bar in DC, has "one drink" and finds himself a drinking buddy. The next morning, one bar fight, one gash requiring stitches in his right hand, and a jail visit stand between him and the prayer breakfast.

Fortunately B.J. posts his bail, and the long, embarrassing train ride home gets Jim thinking. Home means alone with the demons. A different feeling than shame is just a drink and a snort away. "Sure," a voice says. "Shake hands with your old friends, booze and blow." It's like being friends with a pair of vipers. Every time you reach for it, you end up bitten, bruised, or bleeding. And Jim just keeps on reaching.

It's like being friends with a pair of vipers. Every time you reach for it, you end up bitten, bruised, or bleeding. And Jim just keeps on reaching.

A couple nights later, Jim's home alone, high, with self-loathing killing his buzz. The phone rings. It's B.J. He agrees to meet Jim at the emergency room to take care of the hand.

No words are exchanged at the ER for a long time. Finally B.J. asks, "Can I pray for you?"

"Yeah."

"Okay." B.J. nods. "All right. Repeat after me." A calm assurance carries his words through Jim's haze, and with four simple sentences, Jim Muzikowski surrenders control of his life to Jesus Christ.

But for what purpose?

Fast forward. In 1988, Jim and his wife and family move to Chicago adjacent to the infamous Cabrini-Green housing projects. Checkerboard concrete high-rises that are the caricature of urban blight. Violent crime, prostitution, fatherlessness, innocent victims, and hopelessness. Jim's friends at work can't believe he lives just a few blocks away and are even more shocked to learn that he jogs through the neighborhood in the early dawn hours. Cabrini-Green is not home to much hope, but Jim keeps eyeing a patch of urban landscape that has two backstops standing as monuments to days gone by when the kids in the neighborhood caught baseballs and hit homers. Now the kids catch stray rounds from handguns and get hit with loss after loss.

A repeated thought. A prompting. A leading. A crazy dream for God continues to knock on the door of Jim's mind and heart. There it is again: *The kids in this neighborhood could use a real Little League to play in.* Over and over again the tape plays, and the scene unfolds in his mind of clean fields, pinstriped uniforms, smiles, and laughs. It's absurd, and everyone tells him so. "Liberal white do-gooders" are all talk, but eventually a man named Al Carter, a baseball coach, finally gets it that this might be more than an empty vision.

Jim goes to Williamsport, Pennsylvania, applies, and Near North Little League is approved. He and an army of volunteers help clear the fields of debris and trash. The City of Chicago pitches in. The Secretary of State pulls a few strings to get the lights turned back on. Committees are formed. Fliers are printed and posted in all the parochial and public schools. Sign-up dates are selected.

Nine in the morning on sign-up day, Jim and his wife are the only people there. By eleven there are a few kids and their moms. Jim starts hitting grounders and telling whoever's interested to grab some of the gloves he brought. A crowd forms around the table, and by midafternoon there's a line down the block. And the rest, as the Spirit would say, is "His-story."

Two hundred and fifty kids sign up to play baseball in the first season of the Near North Little League, twenty teams in two age groups. Word gets out, and every major television network visits, Jim is given a Points of Light Award by the first Bush administration, spin-off community programs are started, college scholarships are initiated, and thousands of players', families', and volunteers' lives are changed as a result of one man's decision to become the solution.

Why'd he do it?

Jim says, "For my part, I can say it was because I loved God, kids, and baseball. I wanted to be a good neighbor. I wanted to do the next right thing. After all, somebody coached me when I was growing up."[1]

Loaves and Fish

Great thoughts—the ones that are selfless—are from God. Jim Muzikowski was neither the most selfless nor sharpest tool on God's workbench to start with, but Jesus Christ rebuilt him from the inside out. With a rebuilt heart and mind, new insight, new purposes, and new plans came into a recovering alcoholic's mind that shocked and excited him. Nurtured with faith, those great thoughts for God, combined with faithful actions, produced great results that brought great glory to God. It's *so* like Jesus to take our little and make more.

> When Jesus looked up and saw a great crowd coming toward him, he said to Philip, "Where shall we buy bread for these people to eat?" He asked this only to test him, for he already had in mind what he was going to do.
>
> Philip answered him, "Eight months' wages would not buy enough bread for each one to have a bite!"
>
> Another of his disciples, Andrew, Simon Peter's brother, spoke up. "Here is a boy with five small barley loaves and two small fish, but how far will they go among so many?"
>
> Jesus said, "Have the people sit down." (John 6:5–10)

Philip gives Jesus a mouthful. The boy gives Jesus a sack full. Andrew remains doubtful. Way to go, boys; no gold stars for you today. *That* one goes to the seven-year-old who saw and heard a need, came to Jesus, and gave what he had. Tell a little kid you can't afford to sponsor a Compassion child and she comes back holding up her piggy bank. Children don't know what it costs and they don't care. They're just focused on a solution.

Of such is the kingdom, Jesus said. Jim Muzikowski got it, and so can we. God's man does not require full knowledge before he starts obeying the Lord's will. This is called aggressive faith.

A young pastor moves to California. God has given him promptings, leadings, thoughts, visions of a church that will meet the needs of thousands of people and influence the world. What are his loaves and fish? Let's see, he's got a small U-Haul and a couple hundred bucks. No house, no congregation, and no funding. He and his wife decide to leave all that up to God as they pull into town and stop at the first real estate office they encounter. He walks in. He tells his story. He walks out with a new place, the first two months rent free and his first congregation member! This is 1980.

Twenty-five years later, this same pastor takes the stage at Angel Stadium in Anaheim, California, before a congregation of thirty thousand to celebrate what God did with some loaves and fish back in 1980. His name is Rick Warren. And while the world may have gotten to know this God's man in the last several years as the leader of the Purpose Driven Movement and the Global PEACE Plan, he is still the guy he was in 1980. He just simply keeps giving Jesus what he has, not knowing what all will happen, and allowing Jesus to multiply what he's got into more for His purposes. He is the man God has chosen to meet a certain need for the kingdom from where he has been placed.

The twist of the loaves-and-fish event with the disciples is that Jesus already knew what He was going to do before He launched the whole process. He was obviously ready to do it. And obviously He knew He was fully capable of doing it on His own. "Have the people sit down" was not a request so much as it was an expression of complete mastery, control, and ability. Yet He enjoined Grumpy (Philip) and used the situation to involve and *test* His men. He wanted them to participate.

It's like when I wash the family SUV in our driveway. It's my idea and agenda. I pull out all the cleaning supplies, unfurl the hose, attach the Turbo Nozzle, turn on the water, scrub the rims, spray and squeegee the glass, buff the interior, polish the tires, shammy it, vacuum it, and put it all away.

That's the job. Yet inevitably my kids come outside and ask: "Dad, can I help?" as one of them clutches my Turbo Nozzle and squeezes the trigger. If I am lucky, they may complete a rim or fender. With every car wash event:

- The original plan is mine.
- I want my kids to participate.
- I know who's gonna do the heavy lifting.
- The process is fun and we connect.
- They do what they can.
- I do what only I can.
- I make sure the job is completed to my satisfaction.
- The size and scope of detailing an SUV does not overwhelm me but would overwhelm my children if I weren't there.
- When I am involved, my kids never think: *It's never gonna happen.*

So when it comes to serving God the way He intends, you have to inquire about and seek what it is that God already has on the agenda and get involved in that. If it seems a little bigger than your abilities, then just grab the Turbo Nozzle and squeeze!

Time to Contribute

Jim Muzikowski had natural giftings before he became a believer. He had incredible energy. He had a desire to experience purpose—that elusive "more" urge. He had passion for sports. He had a tender spot for helping kids. He hungered to experience and unleash the power of community. These motivations were providing clues of where he should be serving. The only cause he knew was his own, and he spent all his energy funding the next good feeling.

Then he met a group of people who had their motivations and giftings in sync for a purpose that was greater than themselves. He saw a cause that people were giving their lives to. Everything they did came together for the good of God's kingdom and the people around them God wanted to touch. What I love about Jim's story is that slowly, steadily, surely, his good and bad experiences, his natural talents, his passion for sports, his circumstances, and his connections started coalescing into a dream that only God could fulfill.

This is the greatness every man seeks on earth: to be used in a way greater than himself that makes sense for a cause.

Pastor Rick is my pastor. He likes to say that a man will be most effective when he "uses his *spiritual gifts* and *abilities* in the area of his *heart's desire* and in a way that expresses his *personality* and *experiences.*" This is the greatness every man seeks on earth: to be used in a way greater than himself that makes sense for a cause. This is the definition of a warrior in most cultures. But for this to happen we have to put all that we are in God's hands and give Him the freedom to train, shape, mold, develop, and direct us the way He intends. The things we previously used for selfish purposes, we now risk handing over to God for His purposes.

"But Kenny," you say, "how do I *know* what I'm supposed to contribute?"

Trust God to speak to you through the answers to these questions:

- What are the things I care about most *as a man?*
- What's my natural skill set?
- Where do I get results versus failure?
- What subjects do I love to talk about?
- Where do I like to invest my physical energy?
- In what situations do I find myself getting most competitive?
- What are the core parts of my testimony as a Christian?
- What did I struggle with as a nonbeliever?
- What do I continue to struggle with?
- Where am I most energized spiritually?
- What has been the biggest loss I've ever suffered?
- When did I feel the most pain?
- If I could do anything for God, what would it be?

God will not call you to a specific ministry without having you consider the honest answers to these questions. He wants to use *everything* that you are—not just the pretty pieces but also the painful parts that you don't like to bring up. Authentic manhood versus synthetic manhood is a matter of honesty. When you are honest with God, self, and others, you are a free man: free to serve with all that you are versus wearing masks to hide insecurities. Don't you find it interesting that the best-selling men's books don't talk about inspirational success stories but about battles, inner tensions, conflicts, and overcoming obstacles? I'll talk about this more later, but wherever there are men, there is fertile ministry if you are just honest with yourself and others!

I need to warn you: if you are willing to give God the loaves and fish of your life and ask Him to multiply them, expect resistance.

- You will unnerve the control freaks because you are trusting God.
- You will unsettle the rule follower because you break convention.
- You will anger the cautious because you see a big God leading you.
- You will make traditionalists shake their heads.
- You will anger the cowardly for Christ by raising the bar of faith.
- You will upset the approval freaks because you've stopped depending on others to give you your identity.
- You will move into unknown, obscure, and mysterious waters without knowing all the details.
- You will become a target because you are on the offensive.

As you begin to take more risks and become a solution to the needs around you in the name of your King, God will progressively increase both the scope and the scale of the risks you need to take for Him. Risk for a toddler is jumping into Daddy's arms in the pool. Risk for my ten-year-old is dropping in a quarter pipe at the skate park. Risk for a high-school senior is standing up for what's unpopular. And so on. God will always call you to progressively aggressive faith in step with your growth. He knows just how to stretch us.

If you are willing to give God the loaves and fish of your life and ask Him to multiply them, expect resistance.

As a man who is known for commanding the field and taking risks on the gridiron, football coach Mike Martz also knows the value of taking the narrow road of serving the Lord as God's man. He prays a prayer every God's man needs to pray—he asks for the courage not to take "relatively safe risks" but to take the "go-for-broke-ones."

Think bigger about how God wants to use you.

chapter 6

ruthless pursuit

You cannot become the man you need to be by remaining who you are.

—Scott Hitzel

The submarine USS *Halibut* was as close to stealth technology on the high seas as a WWII vessel could be. It remained unseen under the water, stalking its quarry until its periscope emerged imperceptible with an enemy vessel in its crosshairs. In just nine short months, the crew had become deft stalkers at sea, and they were gaining confidence.

In the winter of early 1943, on its third and fourth patrols off the northeast coast of Japan, the USS *Halibut* netted four sunk ships. It was ambushed by decoy vessels with concealed guns and torpedo tubes, chased by escort ships, and forced to retreat underwater by depth-charge attacks. Yet each time, the quick-thinking *Halibut* crew came up victorious, certain there wasn't much, if anything, that could overpower them.

They had proven they could handle the worst the enemy could dish out.

The *Halibut* began her fifth patrol on June 10, 1943, sailing out of Pearl Harbor toward the island of Truk. On June 23 she had her first of two engagements. The enemy had been located, and the sub was stalking a convoy of ships. The well-oiled crew was poised for the order to surface and unload torpedoes. As in the past the order finally came, sites were selected, ranges were calculated, torpedo tubes were loaded and, on orders, fired.

As the birds flew toward their targets, the captain peered through his periscope, tracking their paths with the movements of the ships. It wasn't an exact science. After all, these were moving targets. On this day the torpedoes closed in, and the captain's heart rate accelerated as in a few seconds he expected to see the unmistakable scene of a hull being ripped apart by one of his torpedoes.

Three, two, one… Nothing. *Huh?*

All the torpedoes had missed their targets, and now, because she'd surfaced, the *Halibut* had been spotted by enemy planes. Immediately an aggressive attack began as planes employed airborne magnetic detectors, signaling the sub's position to the convoy and effectively neutralizing its best defense. As the planes circled overhead, the enemy ships could dial in the sub's exact location and layout a deadly depth-charge pattern. Suddenly the hunter had become the hunted.

Of all the encounters a submariner had to endure, depth-charge attacks were the most unsettling. Depth charges were crude weapons, cans filled with TNT dropped into the water with hydrostatic valves preset to explode at a certain depth. Attacking ships could release several charges in succession from the stern while tactically firing others to form a pattern of width and depth to increase their chance of hitting their target. Most of the time the charges wouldn't hit the submarines, but the explosions could loosen seams, create leaks, and force them to surface.

Chief Petty Office Caryle Hamner heard the horn signaling an immediate dive, but the planes were right on top of them, directing their volleys of depth charges with deadly accuracy.

Two hundred feet. Boom!

Two twenty-five. Boom!

Hamner was not a seasoned submariner, but he knew they were in serious jeopardy. As the sub kept diving to get out of range, a scenario started to play out in Hamner's mind.

If we can't control the damage, we'll have to surface. And we have no torpedoes left. Faced with this reality, Hamner said a silent prayer. *Lord, is this it? Are we going to die in this watery grave?*

Then, in the midst of the noise and fear, Hamner remembered something. He ran to his locker and found his daily devotional. Boom! He leafed through the book to find the scripture and message for June 23. Boom! He read the Bible passage for the day, Isaiah 43:2: "When thou passest through the waters, I will be with thee" (KJV).

Below the passage it said: "When thou comest to the waters, thou shalt not go down but through." He scanned it again slowly, and the words hit his heart. "Thou shalt not go down *but through*."

He looked up and realized he'd received his answer. Here, in the moment of his greatest crisis, with almost certain destruction upon them, the words of God found their way to his heart. Suddenly, another sort of depth charge went off inside Chief Petty Officer Hamner, exploding his fears and replacing them with a powerful faith.

Boom! God had spoken.

With a newfound peace, Hamner placed the book back in his locker and returned to his post. Thundering blasts continued to rattle the sub, but his fear was replaced with a quiet confidence. The fear had completely dissolved. God's promise outweighed the circumstances. A loving hand was on him.

The *Halibut* continued diving to a depth of 362 feet—twelve feet beyond its tested rating of 350—and waited out the attack. Finally, the captain gave orders to surface.

Two hundred fifty feet. Nothing.

One hundred fifty feet. Nothing.

Fifty feet. Silence.

A periscope pierced the surface, and the captain surveyed the stormy water. The crew held their breaths as he searched the area. Suddenly, the captain made an announcement, and a cheer went up among the men. They had emerged in the middle of a huge storm—the perfect cover! The planes, unable to see in the midst of the tempest, had been forced to move on. Can you imagine the relief? The celebration that must have followed on the ride home?

With green lights all around and not an enemy ship in sight, the fifth patrol continued on with their mission, eventually returning safely to Midway Island with another hair-raising story to share.

Indeed, the *Halibut* and her crew had made it *through.*

The Battlefield of Coasting

Many of us have stories of God's supernatural intervention and reassurance in times of fear. As God's men, we will know this kind of battle pressure if we are on the attack and serving Him on kingdom battlefronts. As with the *Halibut,* there may come a time when we'll be hammered by circumstances, springing leaks, and forced to the surface to face the assault after some aspect of our character has been compromised. Having fought and won some major battles for the kingdom, God's men commonly become overconfident in our successes. At these times, the challenge is continuing to work *through* the stages of our spiritual journeys, allowing God to direct us to our next missions.

If there is one aspect of spiritual battle that remains more hidden than others among Christian leaders, it is coasting. The thought goes like this: *I can become the man God needs me to be by remaining who I am.* In this realm, the danger is not doing wrong, it is the pride that comes with doing all the right things. When you have a large, level area of the spiritual high ground, you can lose your focus on the real world.

Is this you?

- I am spending time in the Word and prayer.
- I am accountable and sexually pure.
- I am committed to my wife and family.
- I am working with other men.
- I am tithing and giving.
- I am a leader in my church.
- I am pursuing ministry.

If you have most of these things going for you, great! But even if you had them all down pat, you'd still be in danger. Doing all the right works isn't the point. The question is: *Now what?* Once you've "conquered" all those, where do you go from there?

Ironically, spiritual success is the ultimate *test, since the Enemy never simply lies down and gives up just because you've got a good spiritual routine going.*

The fact is that growth, spiritual expansion, victory, and exciting new experiences in Christ await. And they will create a whole new level of spiritual battle. This new foe will not be looking so much to exploit your failure as to get you resting on your success. Few men are prepared for this new character test. Ironically, spiritual success is the *ultimate* test, since the Enemy never simply lies down and gives up just because you've got a good spiritual routine going.

Instead, he throws in a few depth charges. "Hey," he says,

- "You have balance now. Everything's great right here at the status quo. No need to push so hard anymore and keep fighting and risking so much. Wouldn't it be better just to stop being so aggressively spiritual?"
- "You're far too busy to go over there tonight. You don't have time to be Joe Super Christian anymore. Look, you're in a hurry all the time; you just can't have such demanding relationships with God or people right now."
- "You are absolutely amazing. Look at your exploits for God! So much accomplished in such a little time—you really have a gift for this. They're lucky to have you."

Getting the picture? If you're a pastor, Satan might use your successful ministry style to help you avoid the hard questions about your spiritual health as a leader. Or he can use the people around you to convince you to value recognition over true servant leadership and solid character. But sooner or later, if you're coasting, you're going to encounter some devilish sabotage. The only defense is to accept that difficult growth always requires ruthless pursuit of God. Anything less leaves you vulnerable.

Remember, you will never "arrive" until you arrive. As in, "Hello, Jesus, nice place you got here" arrive. The Bible is clear that down here we'll never arrive. We simply keep fighting, becoming more like Christ with every "success," remembering that the only true success is the one that points to Him. Here's how you do it:

- "Just as you received Christ Jesus as Lord, continue to live in him, rooted and built up in him, strengthened in the faith as you were taught, and overflowing with thankfulness" (Colossians 2:6–7). Relentlessly pursue the deeper power—the suboceanic strength beneath the surface of our spiritual lives that makes us seaworthy and ensures our missions are for God. Then leave port again on your next spiritual adventure.

- "Continue to work out your salvation with fear and trembling, for it is God who works in you to will and to act according to his good purpose" (Philippians 2:12–13). We must risk never arriving on this earth but ruthlessly pursue deeper character.
- "Let us examine our ways and test them, and let us return to the LORD" (Lamentations 3:40). We must risk relentless self-examination.
- "He himself bore our sins in his body on the tree, so that we might die to sins and live for righteousness" (1 Peter 2:24). We must risk a ruthless elimination of sin and cultivate holiness.
- "But I'll take the hand of those who don't know the way, who can't see where they're going. I'll be a personal guide to them, directing them through unknown country. I'll be right there to show them what roads to take, make sure they don't fall into the ditch" (Isaiah 42:16, MSG). We must risk relentless trust in God to personally take us through seasons of difficult growth in order to avoid coasting or falling away.

There are times in our lives when training, gifting, and desire will not take us where we need to be as God's men. Sometimes only some objective, brutal honesty will suffice. And while the foolish may "succeed" without acknowledging sin and faults, God's man always knows he has, in the famous words of Yoda, "much to learn."

This Is Gonna Hurt

I call my co-worker Tom Chapin on his cell. "Tom, did you eat lunch already?"

"No."

"You and Danny want to meet me at Pick Up Stix? I'm starving."

"We'll see you there."

Right on. I badly need to connect and catch up with these guys. I haven't seen either of them for months following a writing project and vacation.

I get to the restaurant first, find a table outside, and start making calls until they arrive. I'm feeling great, everything cool, situation normal. Meanwhile, Tom and Danny are shaking in their pants, not letting on that they've been planning to have "a talk" with me—about *me.*

They indulge me, ask how I'm doing, and suffer through a few stories about research for the new book. I talk and talk and talk while they eat. Suddenly I stop. "Hey, I'm doing all the talking. How are you guys doing?"

Danny swallows and puts down his fork. "Kenny, this is going to be a hard conversation for you."

Just like that, the music stopped. The chewing stopped. My heart rate seemed to kick it up a notch. Danny looked down. Tom's eyes were a bit damp.

Oh no. Something was coming. I just didn't know what.

For the next two hours Tom and Danny lovingly but painstakingly performed spiritual heart surgery on their friend and boss. I played the comatose patient, shocked into silence, totally caught off guard, sinking to new depths of disbelief, since I'm the kind of guy who makes sure he's never caught off guard. This was a full-court press spiritual intervention. Their message—and embarrassingly accurate examples—couldn't have been clearer: *You have a major blind spot, buddy, and it's pride!*

I felt as if my heart had been ripped out and they were playing catch with it right there in the Chinese restaurant. They were totally exposing the guy that only *I* could know privately at such deep, subconscious levels. It was all-out, guts-and-entrails freaky. Just minutes earlier, I was feeling as good about my walk with the Lord, relationship with Chrissy, and efforts in ministry as a man can feel. And then these guys had the gall to say things to me I had never heard anyone say.

Hard to hear? Triple-root-canal hard.

Difficult to accept? I wanted to defend myself so bad!

Were they right? More than right. I was exposed. They gave me an abrasive bath in the truth about myself and it was not refreshing.

Like two experienced lawyers, they cited chapter and verse of events, conversations, actions, words, which demonstrated I was not walking in humility or honoring the Lord. At one point in the middle of the operation, they asked how I was feeling. All I could come up with was "sucker-punched." I was battling competing thoughts: *They are so right*

I felt as if my heart had been ripped out and they were playing catch with it right there in the Chinese restaurant.

and, *But what about you?* Thankfully, God put the holy clamp to mouth. This was *His* doing. This was not about them. This was *His* ambush. These were *His* men expressing tough love for me as a leader. They were telling me exactly what I needed to hear, and with laserlike accuracy.

Slowly my spirit began to change. I saw God's hand on the scalpel and knew this was going to be used by Him if I'd swallow my pride and get my attitude straight. Sure, I was crushed, but I kept listening—I had to. These were not stabs to kill; they were cuts to heal and help me go to the next level as God's man. The discomfort was actually confirming the need.

At the end of the grueling two-hour surgery, I thanked them. No one had cared enough to talk to me like that in a long time. By God's grace, I realized I'd been so caught up in what *I* was doing, I had lost perspective. But with tears rolling down my face, I prayed with my friends on that restaurant patio and started the process of repentance before God. I knew it would include going to a few select people to ask for forgiveness. It would also involve requesting assistance on a few things I was selfishly guarding for myself. In a sense, Tom and Danny (they call themselves "the two goofballs") risked their jobs and friendships to have that conversation. Deep down, though, they trusted my desire to be God's man would prevail, thank God.

More than anything, God's man wants to be fruitful and knows that, in Christ, pruning is needed.

And thankfully for me, it did.

I think I know a little bit of how Caryle Hamner felt as he began to panic, waiting for that final depth charge. Why he needed God to reassure him.

He needed to know he'd get *through* it and that God was with him in the midst of it all. Just as that promise from Isaiah gave Hamner the confidence and peace to resume his post, God's loving presence kept me from squirming out of His discipline. When I reflected on it later, I was reminded of the connection between fruitfulness and discipline found in the book of Hebrews.

> At the time, discipline isn't much fun. It always feels like it's going against the grain. Later, of course, it pays off handsomely, for it's the well-trained who find themselves mature in their relationship with God. (Hebrews 12:11, MSG)

"Space invading" is a concept we'll return to later, but for now, the point is that God's man believes in the ministry of discomfort. He believes God is behind the temporary discomfort of building greater character and a deeper level of honesty with himself, with God, and in all his relationships. He has trained himself to heed and respond, no matter what personal price must be paid. He's open to correction because he loves Christ more than he loves his image. He wants to make it as far as he can in the school of Christlikeness and refuses to drop out. He wants wisdom and insight more than influence or affluence: "Teach the wise, and they will be wiser. Teach the righteous, and they will learn more" (Proverbs 9:9, NLT). More than anything, God's man wants to be fruitful and knows that, in Christ, pruning is needed.

The day after my conversation with Tom and Danny, they were concerned and asked me how I was doing. I was so happy to have this blind spot pointed out that one could think my response bordered on denial: "I'm doing awesome!" They knew they had done the right thing and that their intervention and surgery was already paying off. The experience reminded me of Stuart Briscoe's comments on spiritual growth when he wrote:

> The cultivated rose, that most fragrant and most beautiful of flowers, has captured the imagination of poets and songwriters down through the centuries. But roses left to themselves soon run wild. They lose their fragrance, the blooms deteriorate, thorns and brambles take over, and no one writes of their beauty. They need the pruner's knife to cultivate them and make them beautiful again.[1]

Might be a wimpy image for some, but for God's men, being a rose in God's garden is a privilege. To be in the place where He goes to be refreshed, to see His efforts in our lives, His character shining through, reflecting His holy aroma, there's something undeniably significant about being a part of it.

Make a break with pride. Become the man God intended you to be by *refusing to remain who you are.*

chapter 7

passionate sons

And what is a man without energy? Nothing—nothing at all.

—MARK TWAIN

Men love commanding a throttle.

When we men need to pass up Grandma, want to lose the competition, or just want to feel the power, we don't consider the consequences—we *gun* it! It's in our DNA. Unfortunately, this quality can drive our relationships with God and people right off a cliff.

Laurence Gonzales is someone who would know about living a full-throttle life. Laurence had the distinction of being an editor at *Playboy* magazine in the seventies. Here's what he said:

> We were on top of the world, making tens of millions a year in pure profit. We had a private DC-9 airliner, limousines, virtually unlimited expense accounts, and anything else we could dream up. There was a Picasso over the fireplace at the mansion, a Dalí in the powder

> room. Editorial meetings with Hefner could run from 1 in the afternoon until 2 in the morning, with meals served by liveried butlers. If things got boring, there was a swimming pool in the basement. One wall was glass and faced a subterranean bar, where we could sit and watch the Playmates swim while we sipped a glass of the house wine, a 1964 Château Lafite Rothschild.
>
> Oh, and we had promiscuous sex and lots of drugs, too.
>
> Our life was an attempt to stay forever in that precious space between desire and pleasure, between wanting and having, switching back and forth from one to the other so quickly that sometimes it was like having an electrode implanted in your brain: Just press the lever for the next rush.
>
> I remember one sunny afternoon, sitting on the edge of a bed in a suite at the mansion and chatting amiably with the next Playmate of the Month, who happened to be naked. And I wondered, *How long can this go on? How much can you want? How much can you have?* I excused myself and walked the tree-lined streets back toward our art deco building on Lake Michigan, and eventually arrived at the ultimate question: Can you have too much fun?[1]

Larry's asking the wrong question, but he's real close. The question isn't, "Can you have too much fun?" The question is, "Can I live at full throttle and be content?" God knows billions of Larrys have asked this question, and His response is always the same: "Let me give you something more permanent."

> Why spend your money on food that does not give you strength? Why pay for food that does you no good? Listen, and I will tell you where to get food that is good for the soul!
>
> Come to me with your ears wide open. Listen, for the life of

> your soul is at stake. I am ready to make an everlasting covenant with you. I will give you all the mercies and unfailing love that I promised to David. (Isaiah 55:2–3, NLT)

Misplaced Passions

God's man is called to invest his passions in the service of life, not invest his life in the service of his passions. God knows that we have energy to devote to something, and He designed that energy to be put toward knowing and loving Him—in worship. Larry's life is a parable of that journey. Unfortunately, he and billions of other men are being deceived, fruitlessly worshiping the wrong things and paying the price. All of us can relate to Larry at some level and connect to his disillusionment. The objects we worship hijack our souls, morph our characters, and transform our conduct. The truth of this is masterfully captured by famed author and alcoholic Raymond Chandler in *The Long Goodbye.* He says about his object of worship, "Alcohol is like love: The first kiss is magic, the second is intimate, the third is routine. After that, you just take the girl's clothes off."

God's man is called to invest his passions in the service of life, not invest his life in the service of his passions.

Sadly, millions of Christian men are experiencing a similar letdown with God. We start off in awe and "magic" as salvation invades our soul. But slowly our spiritual high is tempered by some of the realities of spiritual growth that are going to have to be worked out rather than "magically" resolved. We experience what an addict would call a "buzz kill" and come off our high. We are disillusioned. Slowly but surely our walk with God becomes familiar and routine. The raging fire has dwindled to a tiny ember that doesn't provide light or comfort to those around it. We are simply going through the motions and begin to look toward other outlets to be passionate about. What happened to our worship? our passion?

Fact time: Our relationships reveal what's wrong with our worship. Polluting your worship of Christ is Satan's goal, and he will try to infect it by introducing worldly desires to increase, indulge, and impress. He wants to put sand in the gas tank of your spiritual life and tube your relationships with God and people. He will work hard to get you to blend worldly passions into the fabric of your godliest passions. It's subtle, but here's why you have to be diligent.

Materialists are bad at relationships because they worship inanimate objects without souls or emotions. My Mercedes and my money can't give me a hug, laugh, cry, or be hurt by my stupidity. Things are safe to love because they require no character but unsafe for your soul because they are soulless. So don't worship things or begin to be more concerned about money and things you own (or don't) than about God and people. Ask: *Am I in bondage to credit-card bills? Am I tithing regularly? Am I being generous? Am I trying to impress others by what I drive or wear? Am I being a good steward of God's money? Am I obsessing over a toy?* This is a heart adjustment. Clean out your carburetor.

Satan is a crooked mechanic, always looking to pop the hood of our spiritual lives and mess around.

Hedonists are bad at relationships because they pimp people, seeing them ultimately as objects of or a means of achieving self-gratification. Nobody I have ever known loves being prostituted for someone else's high. Don't worship "feelings" or physical sensations or risky behaviors because, if you do, you will end up addicted to something and enslaved to it. Satan wants your God to become the reward center in your brain called the ventral tegmental area (VTA), which releases dopamine. He wants you to worship that release and ritual behavior leading up to it. Ask: *Am I searching for stuff on TV? Am I addicted to sexual Happy Meals? Am I loving my wife? Am I enslaved by lustful thoughts and masturbation? Do I have an attachment to any activity that is hurting my walk with God or my relationships? Am I using any behavior as a substitute for real intimacy with God or people? Is my number one temptation becoming my number one solution?* This is an emotional intimacy adjustment. Change the oil.

Narcissists are bad at relationships too because—you guessed it—it's all about them! A relational narcissist is an oxymoron. Not so surprisingly, I've met quite a few pastors in this category. Relationships these men form with people are not relationships at all, they are mirrors designed to reflect back on them in a positive way—or else. You can't love yourself, your appearance, your titles, and your control over others and genuinely serve someone else's needs. Ask: *Am I responsible for my success or is God? Am I better than other people? Is it hard for me to take advice from people? Am I a good listener? Am I in touch with the needs of those around me or aloof?* This is an ego adjustment. Replace the filter.

Satan is a crooked mechanic, always looking to pop the hood of our spiritual lives and mess around. He suggests maintenance we don't need so he can profit. He will dress it up in different ways with a powerful presentation. He likes hoodwinking God's men because he knows that pursuers of power, enthusiastic indulgers, and men passionate about possessions share one common denominator: a low view of people and a broken relationship with God.

Consider:

- There are twenty-five million prostitutes who wake up each day and are gainfully employed by men who don't have the character to do real relationships.
- There are fourteen million orphans in Africa who are the sons and daughters of men who left their villages to work elsewhere, slept with prostitutes, contracted HIV AIDS, came back, and infected their wives.
- In the urban cities of America between 60 and 70 percent of the families have no father living in the household.
- There's a network television show called *Cheaters* dedicated to the lack of moral character in men, which identifies and exposes husbands by catching them in the act.
- Fifty-seven billion dollars is spent on pornography annually in the world. Seventy-five to 80 percent of those dollars come out of men's bank accounts or show up on men's credit-card statements.
- In many Third World and impoverished countries, we have government-sponsored training programs for maids who are sent abroad to earn money and send it back to their families to pump up the economy, but many never return because they are abused and murdered by their male employers.
- In Singapore and Thailand, there is a thriving child-prostitution enterprise marketed to Western men, which is making millions annually.

Instead of investing in food for our souls (loving God back and loving others), the culture around us inspires us to crave everything else, and our impact on the world becomes pathetic. Misplaced passions. Idol worship. Broken lives. Lost legacies. This is not the kind of worship and leadership we are called to in the world.

A Full-Throttle Father

God's a dad. You are a son. Never forget it.

Every dad who is connected to his son has a special relationship. Dads rejoice when sons they love reproduce their own best and noblest qualities. Similarly, dads lament over sons when they don't see their values and character reproduced in their boys. If you are a dad, you know exactly what I am talking about. As a son, you probably sense it too.

God's expectations are high because we are His boys. More often than not in the Bible, God was gravely disappointed when He checked in on the boys. During Isaiah's day He checked in: "The vineyard of the LORD Almighty is the house of Israel, and the men of Judah are the garden of his delight. And he looked for justice, but saw bloodshed; for righteousness, but heard cries of distress" (Isaiah 5:7). In this "Song of the Vineyard," God talks about His affection for His people, singling out His men. As the chapter continues, it describes a culture of men whose passion for God has been polluted. It seems materialism, addiction, sexual conquest, and being two-faced spiritually were as prevalent then as they are today. Forget gassing the throttle for the Lord; these guys couldn't even start their engines for Him. We may often forget God is this interested in us, but this passage along with another in Jeremiah (which I discuss on the next page) is emphatic about how He feels about you right now—as a son.

You are "the garden of his delight." A garden is a place to sow and go to enjoy what you've sown. A garden is a place of refreshment, color, and beauty that ministers to us. It is a place of productivity and fruitfulness. To God, you represent the possibility of all these things.

He wants to see His work in you. When God goes to visit the garden of His delight, He's on the hunt for something very specific: "He looked for justice…for righteousness." His father's heart can't help it. He wants to see the character traits of compassion, goodness, and godliness being reproduced in you.

The people connected to your life tell Him the story. When He checks in on us, He's closely examining the substance of our relationships. The scorecard in Isaiah's day suggests the men of Judah did not pass the character test, which means they would fail the relationship test. God heard the "cries of distress" and saw the "bloodshed" His boys were producing in others' lives and was grieved. The landscape of His sons' lives was littered with broken relationships because of a callousness to God's Spirit, wreaking havoc on the nation. They not only let Satan look under the hood, they were handing him wrenches!

Forget gassing the throttle for the Lord; these guys couldn't even start their engines for Him.

You are the family ambassador to improve the world. Sound overblown? Listen to this: " 'If you will…return to me. If you put your detestable idols out of my sight and no longer go astray, and if in a truthful, just and righteous way you swear, "As surely as the LORD lives," then the nations will be blessed by him and in him they will glory.' This is what the LORD says to the men of Judah and to Jerusalem: 'Break up your unplowed ground and do not sow among thorns. Circumcise yourselves to the LORD, circumcise your hearts, you men of Judah' " (Jeremiah 4:1–4). This is a textbook "come to Jesus" meeting with His boys. Why the energy? Why the passion? Why the focus on their worship of God alone? Answer:

His purposes of advancing in the world depended on it. Want to feel real power? Just pop the hood and let the Master mechanic have His way.

So what's under the hood of your spiritual life? A kitty or a viper? Does your spiritual engine perform or sputter when you hit the throttle? Do you feel His power propelling you past your shortcomings, through your difficulties, and into health in your relationships? Or do you feel like you're driving Auntie Eleanor's '64 Falcon stuck in first gear? God is looking for a full-throttle man—a man who worships God with his very life.

Jesus looked forward to a day when the passions and energy of men would be fully and unashamedly deployed for God's purposes. He told a woman to watch for this day. "Yet a time is coming and has now come when the true worshipers will worship the Father in spirit and truth, for they are the kind of worshipers the Father seeks. God is spirit, and his worshipers must worship in spirit and in truth" (John 4:23–24).

Here's how to be a full-throttle God's man:

1. *Come home.* Job number one: "Return to me." Put on your signal and make a big fat U-turn!
2. *Quit waffling!* For the men of Judah, this required a recommitment to worshiping Him alone. "Put your detestable idols out of my sight and no longer go astray" is as direct as you can get. No more two-timing God.
3. *Commit sincerely.* The men had made promises to God in the past and broken them, so this time He's asking for integrity by requiring an oath from the heart. "If in a truthful, just and righteous way you swear, 'As surely as the LORD lives'" was God's way of saying posers

and actors will not be tolerated. No more game playing. I want a man who will risk being undivided between what he believes, says, thinks, and acts.

4. *Become a blessing.* This was not a self-improvement program. The world was hanging in the balance based on these men's decisions to make a strong spiritual commitment. The end game of this renewal among God's men was a different world: "Then the nations will be blessed by [God]."

If we take God's Word seriously, this admonition from Jeremiah should hit every God's man like a spiritual overhand right. It should knock us right on our cans. And then as we shake our heads to clear them, we should come out fighting with a renewed purpose, risking a warrior's commitment to worshiping Jesus alone. If you really get this, the "old you" should stay on the canvas for a ten count while the new man bounces across the ring with his arms in the air!

God's man shows extravagant respect for God by living passionately and purposefully for God alone. In other words, do not, at any price, pollute your worship by trying to mix your values, the world's values, or the devil's lies with God's character and God's truth.

God wants to give you the spiritual horsepower to leave your old life in the dust if you'll open up the throttle for Him and not look back. He guarantees it. "By his mighty power at work within us, he is able to accomplish infinitely more than we could ever dare to ask or hope" (Ephesians 3:20, NLT). It doesn't matter whether you are in need of an engine replacement, new muffler, carburetor, gas line, piston, spark plug, or lube and oil change. God has promised that if you wheel your rig into His shop, the sparks will fly, and so will your spiritual life. The question is: Can you handle this much spiritual power?

My advice? Take a risk, accelerate your worship and commitment to Jesus in every way, and see what He can do for you under the hood. You will not be disappointed. In fact, as you see other competitors for your affections and energy fade away in the dust, you'll break into a huge grin. And pretty soon, you'll stop even thinking about looking back.

Be a passionate son.

chapter 8

same is not the enemy

A little in this world will content a Christian for his passage.
—Jeremiah Burroughs

Comparison kills my contentment. The problem is, I have been trained to love new and to despise same.

Billions of dollars are spent by advertisers every year to tell me one thing: be discontent and dissatisfied with your life. It doesn't matter if I am making minimum wage or megamoney, the message is that "more" whatever it is, newer and better, is around the corner and waiting. And so I chase "it" just as long as it is new and makes me feel new. I buy things I don't need with money I don't have to impress people I don't even know. New is the hero, and same is the villain.

I hear the voice of the guy who does all the commercials ringing in my head. You know him. He starts convincing us by asking the same question over and over. "Aren't you tired of your old…" Broom? Dish soap? TV tray? Acne medication? Diet plan? Weed Wacker?

This is the hook and I'm the large-mouth bass.

Porsche dealers, adult bookstores, Sharper Image—even your local marriage counselor—are all in business and going strong because of men's insatiable bent toward "new." The mentality corrodes and eventually erodes our satisfaction with what God has called us to keep, cultivate, and be thankful for.

All over the globe we men have ants in our pants over the same job/account balance/neighborhood/car/routines/church/commute/house/friends/body. We're bored with our wives and bored with our lives. Don Miller's honesty about his own war with "same" strikes a chord with me. It's as if he's seen my movie.

> I like new things too much. I like the way they smell. Today I tried to go to Home Depot to get an extension cord. I need an extension cord to plug in a lamp in the upstairs den. I already bought a timer plug for the lamp, a plug that turns the lamp on in the evening and off after everybody has gone to bed, but now I need an extension cord....
>
> The thing about the extension cord is I was pretty sure I already had one in the basement, in a box with some other cords, but if I looked I might have found it, and then I would not have been able to go to Home Depot. What we needed was a new extension cord, the latest technology....
>
> The thing about new things is you feel new when you buy them, you feel as though you are somebody different because you own something different. We are our possessions, you know. There are people who get addicted to buying new stuff. Things. Piles and

> piles of things. But the new things become old things so quickly. We need new things to replace old things.
>
> I like things with buttons.[1]

What makes you feel new?

A lot of men I talk to would replace Don's "buttons" with "breasts." Sexual discontent is the male parable in a nutshell. We want what we can't have. We think about what we don't have. We dwell on how very much we need it. We forget about what we already have. We talk ourselves into having it. We take action to possess it. We desire an experience with the objects of our affection. We find temporary satisfaction. We loathe the fact that it didn't change a thing or only marginally improved things. We are still the same men with the same problems, just poorer. We remain discontent and frustrated.

> ***Sexual discontent is the male parable in a nutshell. We want what we can't have.***

In the summer of 2005, I was in London and fulfilled a lifelong dream of visiting the prestigious British Museum. During my tour I found myself planted in front of a sign that read:

> Secular Life in the Middle Ages

Below it, a description:

> Trade, feasting, and warfare dominated secular life in the Middle Ages.

Man-world hasn't changed much. New possessions, insatiable appetites, and new power over others have been consuming male passions for centuries. The game was being played then just the same as it is today. We still confuse net worth and self-worth, trade character for gratification, seek power through position. Meanwhile, the people in our lives—or in our way—suffer in the wake of our pursuit of "new" and "more."

What would happen if more of us would risk:

- contentment over consumption?
- satisfaction over searching for more?
- more gratitude over meaningless gratification?
- resting in what we have over restlessness in what we lack?
- connecting with the Joneses over competing with them?
- giving more money to God's work over getting a new toy?
- careers for a cause?
- having less on earth for more in heaven?

Do any of these come naturally to you? Me neither. I need new desires. I need God to change my heart. I need to grow. I need to start risking the superficial for the supernatural.

His Will Be Done

We are here to complete a mission—His mission. There is a myth that God's man must reject and defeat in his own heart, the one that says: you are here to complete *your* mission. This is the Guadalcanal of the spiritual life—His plan or mine? The world and the devil offer us a menu of identities and connected missions that distract God's man from the original plan. Under these deceptions, we are free to use our resources as we choose. We're also free to complain in anger and bitterness about our losses and broken dreams.

The turning point in this battle comes when we risk embracing God's purpose in what we lack; more specifically, when we allow our character to be shaped through contentment with less rather than constantly devoting our time, thoughts, and God-given talents to acquiring stuff.

In God's plan, less does not necessarily mean poverty and more does not necessarily mean wealth—each represents something different to every man depending on his situation. However, contentment does mean that a condition of the heart that preserves God's best is happening in and through you wherever He has called you to be, and with whatever He has called you to have. That is why contentment means something unique to every man and is something every God's man is supposed to pray for. Agur was a man courageous enough to pray such a prayer. He put it to God this way:

> O God, I beg two favors from you before I die. First, help me never to tell a lie. Second, give me neither poverty nor riches! Give me just enough to satisfy my needs. For if I grow rich, I may deny you and say, "Who is the LORD?" And if I am too poor, I may steal and thus insult God's holy name. (Proverbs 30:7–9, NLT)

Every God's man needs to pray this exact prayer! It takes maturity and spiritual grit to pray, but the risk is worth it. Why? Because Agur's prayer strikes at the real issue: preserving his walk with God. He's not worried about anything else except the spiritual mission God has called him to and the character he needs to complete it. Notice he's not holding on to his own plan for himself. He's wide open to God's will for him. What matters most to this God's man is God's plan for his life coming about and preserving his heart commitment to that plan. This guy knows his shortcomings and what could happen without financial balance. He asks to be delivered from the God-dishonoring dangers in both poverty *and* wealth.

> Lord, give me what you think I need to accomplish your purposes, not what I think I need.

I have experienced both sides of Agur's prayer. There have been times in my life when I have concentrated so much on what I don't have that I have failed to enjoy what I do have. During these times I was less joyful, discontent, and, to my shame, largely ungrateful. It's draining to be a man who always focuses on what he doesn't have, and in the process I stagnated spiritually.

On the other hand, I have had times of financial abundance as an executive, flush with financial bonuses, raises, and promotions. In those times, it was tempting to think that I was the author of my own success. I prayed less, became less dependent on God and more worldly in my focus. In both circumstances, I learned a lot about myself. Namely, that the issue wasn't the amount of money in my bank account, it was about what my character could and could not handle. This is the bottom line on contentment.

Why would God give me a ton of money if the result would be His displacement from the center of my life? Why would God not meet my basic needs (as opposed to wants) if He knew this lack would set me up to fall into sin? I am so glad that Agur's prayer can be mine and yours so that God can bring us to a place of influence for Him no matter what our social or financial status. He's never been big on those anyway. If we are bold enough to pray Agur's prayer, God will bring us to that place of character and contentment that allows us to be used in the way He intends. We move beyond materialism to mission. A poor man may focus on the spiritual gifts, ministry, and people he has influenced, and become spiritually rich. The wealthy man may focus on stewarding his monetary affluence for God's purposes to also become spiritually rich. Contentment redefines "rich." Rich in God. Rich in relationships. Rich in living out His purposes wherever we are and in whatever we do.

Contentment redefines "rich." Rich in God. Rich in relationships. Rich in living out His purposes wherever we are and in whatever we do.

At some point God will call you out on the issue of contentment. Like Agur, we must be willing to risk it all and say to Him:

- Protect me from lies about what's mine and what I deserve.
- Forgive me for believing the lies.
- Give me what I need to keep me faithful to You.
- Help me discern true needs versus wants.
- Help me be grateful for what I have.
- Help me say no to myself so that I can say yes to You.
- Help me use what You give me to glorify God.
- Make me a good steward of Your money.
- Loosen the grip of materialism in my life by making me a giver.
- Help me tithe regularly and joyfully to Your work according to Your Word.

The man who can pray this prayer and act on it is free.

Gratitude and Contentment

Here's a helpful reality: it is impossible to be *thankfully* discontent.

Think about it for second. Have you ever met a thankful complainer? A grateful whiner? A content materialist? These combinations are not possible. The key is developing that attitude of gratitude that leads you out of the tar pits of discontentment.

Jim Burns is a friend of mine who was preaching in our church one Sunday. I had no idea what he was going to talk about, so when I received the bulletin from the usher, I quickly opened it and saw the title of his message: "Thankfulness." The rest of the insert normally used for taking notes on the sermon was blank. By the end of his message both sides of my little page were filled with notes. His challenge to the whole congregation was to begin each day by thanking God for at least twenty-five things—this was supposed to be our "thank therapy." He promised this would change not only our level of contentment but also our character.

It is impossible to be thankfully discontent.

At the time, I was commuting to work, so I decided to test out thank therapy as soon as I got into the car to drive to work instead of flipping on news radio. Much of my willingness to try this admittedly cheesy-sounding approach came from something close to home. I was struggling to be thankful in our finances because Chrissy and I had made cataclysmic changes in our budget to clear all open debt from our family books.

Chrissy was the architect of this austere plan, and I was definitely chafing from the financial friction it was imposing on my personal freedom as the man of the house. I could not do what I wanted. I was packing lunches to take to work, having more dinners in, clipping coupons for everything, cutting out Starbucks, and on and on ad infinitum (that's Latin for "lots"). Withdrawals from the ATM required joint committee meetings. Every available cent was going toward erasing our debt. No exceptions. I knew it had to be done, but I certainly wasn't happy about it.

Enter thank therapy.

Thank You, God, for my car. Thank You for this coffee. Thank You, God, for Chrissy. Thank You for Cara, Ryan, and Jenna. Thank You for this bran muffin. Thank You, God, for a paycheck and providing for my needs. Thank You for this day. Thank You for my church. Thank You for your Word. You get the picture. I tried to be sincere but on some days things would get desperate and I would find myself thanking God for *The Tonight Show* or the Endangered Species Act or a good burp. But I persevered, and after a week or so I did notice that my private whining and complaining outbursts were strangely absent.

After a few weeks of this discipline I was happier about the fact that we were being totally obedient to God with our tithing and debt removal. I was enjoying my sack lunch immensely. I loved hearing how much Chrissy was saving through clipping coupons. I appreciated my old car that had a lot of miles on it. Homemade coffee was just fine and saving me a boatload of cash. Outings with the family cost less and were more creative. We went to the beach a ton that summer for fun. Cheap was chic in south Orange County.

Instead of all that I was being denied, Jim's simple spiritual exercise opened my eyes to all that I had and helped me enjoy those people and things ten times more. But it entailed the risk of going against how I felt at the time (robbed of the little extra indulgences) and doing what the Bible says, "Give thanks in all circumstances, for this is God's will for you in Christ Jesus" (1 Thessalonians 5:18). Notice it doesn't say give thanks *for* everything but give thanks *in* everything.

That was the big lesson for me. I wasn't thankful *for* the mess I was in financially, but because God can use all things, I could be thankful *in* my circumstances for lots of things. I am not thankful *for* the congestive heart failure that killed my dad or the cancer that got my mom. But *in* that season of their lives, I was thankful that God used it to give me a chance to connect with them in ways I never would have otherwise.

This is a mystery to me. A self-sufficient or prideful heart fuels discontentedness and broken relationships with God and people. But gratitude leads to contentment if we are thankful as God commands.

Contentment, Character, and the Cause

I love our house. I am supremely happy and blessed to have a "tent" like ours to camp in while on earth. But every house has its issues, if you know what I mean.

This will seem trivial, but for the sake of transparency I'll confess it: I hate the shower in my bedroom. I am not a huge guy. I am a little over six feet tall, pushing two hundred pounds. But I feel crammed into this thing. Every time I step into it, I knock something over. I hit my elbows against the walls. I bump the door open which lets in all the cold air, which I know makes me sound like a wuss, but the bottom line is that I love taking long hot showers to unwind from the day, and my cramped shower prevents that great "spa" moment of relaxation. The only way that works is to fold my arms across my body and stand exactly in the middle, motionless.

For the last year or so, I had been drawing my dream shower on napkins and pieces of paper. I was talking to some tiling and bathroom remodel guys from church about what it would take to rip out the Jacuzzi tub the previous owners put in (which we never use) in order to make room for a jumbo shower instead. I could see it in my head. I was crunching the numbers, saving up for the blessed day. My dream of a hassle-free shower experience was drawing near, and it was going to be glorious.

Right about that same time, our church was launching a building campaign. You can see it coming, can't you? The junior-high and high-school students were finally going to get their own building. We were getting a new parking lot to accommodate our growing congregation. There would be a bookstore and a variety of other necessary developments and improvements. Each member of the congregation was invited to pray over a three-year financial commitment.

The last time we did a campaign like this, Chrissy and I prayed about what we would commit, came back together, and shared the number God had put on each of our hearts. Since our number had matched exactly that time, I was looking forward to the same process: prayer, stretching our faith, and ultimately a little sacrificing.

As the weekend of commitment drew near, my pastor encouraged me to pray more specifically for the revelation of a number, rather than to reason through our family budget and decide what to give that way. The more I prayed and reflected, the more I saw my new shower plans popping up in my thoughts. I knew God was telling me not to give out of comfort but to sacrifice and be obedient.

I was ready to pull the trigger on that shower. But in my seeking of God's will, I felt led *not* to squeeze that trigger. It may seem stupid to hear, but I was feeling that God wanted me to add the amount the shower would have cost to the number I was originally thinking about committing to the building campaign. Once I had that, I was ready to share my number with Chrissy.

At that moment, an extraordinary sense of contentment and joy came flooding into my soul.

The Saturday night before Commitment Sunday, Chrissy and I were standing in the bathroom, of all places, discussing the dollar amount God had laid on each of our hearts to give over the next three years. I was nervous about telling her my number, afraid it was too big. But I charged ahead and told her my figure. My eyes were trained on her face to gauge her reaction. Her jaw was hanging wide open. Then she exploded: "That's my number too!"

Talk about shock and awe!

We were speechless for a few minutes, and then Chrissy asked, "So how did you get to your number?"

I pointed to the shower and told her I had taken the amount I would have spent on it and added it to my earlier total. She arrived at her number in a totally different way, adding up other sacrifices God had led her to. At that moment, an extraordinary sense of contentment and joy came flooding into my soul. God knew I wanted to do this, but He'd also wanted us to experience a confirmation that would bind Chrissy and me together, realizing all over again His blessing on our lives.

I felt I had done it right. I sensed that the secret to happiness was in simply listening and hearing. That weekend, I made peace with God's purposes over my own. The process made me look at my materialism and reconcile it with my spiritual condition. I was motivated to be content with my old shower for no other reasons than the cause of Christ and to be God's man. I'd had to risk something to gain something, and I wouldn't trade it now for anything.

I am still knocking stuff over in my bedroom shower. My rear still knocks the door wide open so cold air rushes in. My elbows still hit the walls when I am rubbing shampoo into my scalp. But now my reactions are different. I am less bothered, even grateful for that shower because I think about what God taught me through it. I remember how I learned about taking risks to be content for the cause of Christ. It's not about me, thank God. It's about Him and how He wants to use my financial situation to improve my spiritual condition.

What I give is specific to me, and it has to be. It's specific for you too. That's one of the reasons for Paul's description of contentment as a mysterious process between God and His people. It's a secret power given to move us beyond what the world values and into a character free to be thankful and to give abundantly.

No one embodies or expresses this secret power in the Bible better than Paul. As a prisoner in Rome, when he received a care package from his

Philippian friends, he responded by sharing his perspective both on the gift and on how God had worked contentment into his life. You could not fault him if he felt a little bewildered over his imprisonment (John the Baptist felt that way). Instead, we see God's man gushing joy and ministering to people out of a contented heart. Listen closely to a free man in prison.

It's not about me, thank God. It's about Him and how He wants to use my financial situation to improve my spiritual condition.

"I rejoice greatly in the Lord that at last you have renewed your concern for me. Indeed, you have been concerned, but you had no opportunity to show it. I am not saying this because I am in need, for I have learned to be content whatever the circumstances. I know what it is to be in need, and I know what it is to have plenty. I have learned the secret of being content in any and every situation, whether well fed or hungry, whether living in plenty or in want. I can do everything through him who gives me strength" (Philippians 4:10–13).

We've often divorced that last sentence from the body of the thought, but what Paul is saying is that God's man becomes content because of the strength that comes with Christ's perspective. That perspective overcomes concern about your station in life. Both the love of affluence and loathing of poverty become null and void. God's man is free, whatever his situation, when he knows what is eternal. When I am spiritually focused on and connected to Christ, I am:

- more grateful, less stressed
- more focused on God's plan, less focused on my plans

- more interested in people, less interested in things
- more focused on God's purposes in my situation, less focused on what I am missing
- more aware of what is important in life, less concerned with the trivial
- more humble, less prideful

The more risk, the more contentment. The less risk, the more discontentment, entitlement, and self-absorption. God's man is wise to make this connection between the two.

More practically, it's good for us to say no to ourselves sometimes. It's good for us to say no to our kids versus promoting immediate gratification and impulsiveness in their character. It's a good thing for married couples to delay a big purchase, pause a day or two to pray and ask what God wants them to do with His money. It's good for me to say no to some things so I can say yes to God. This is risky business for men who live in a material world, but it is the right risk if you are God's man. We are called to be content. That means, in some cases we will be asked to delay or divert prosperity so that others may experience Jesus's love.

It's good for me to say no to some things so I can say yes to God.

"New" and "more" are okay for some. But for God's man, contentment with "same" has the power to transform you and the people around you for eternity.

chapter 9

Achilles heels

We become God's man when God's grace conquers our fear of others knowing our weaknesses and shortcomings.

—LEVERETT LUCK

Rick Warren nails it when he says, "Sin is fun for a season. You have your kicks. Then you have your kickbacks." The world, our own dark side, and the devil never talk about the kickbacks, only the kicks.

I received a letter from a brother in Christ who felt compelled to give us his view of the other side of sin's results. I get e-mails like this every week. They are heavy and the wounds are still fresh. They are the reflections of men revealing their Achilles heels—their mistakes, failures, and kickback grief. But at the same time, the men are fighting to accept responsibility and truly repent before God.

Dear Kenny,

I imagine that you receive quite a few of these throughout the day so I hope they are not overwhelming or bothersome. My wife was kind enough to purchase me *Every Man, God's Man,* and I have recently read it.

Well, I'll just cut to the chase. I confessed four days ago to an affair I was having. It is destroying my life and I knew it was time to confess so that I could be healed and used for Christ again. My wife wants to divorce me and leave with my two little girls, but thanks to the advice of my pastor, she will not do that at this time. She will wait to see if I change but only upon his request. I feel so broken in my life. To see everything being stripped away is the most painful thing I have endured in my life but I have hope in God. Yesterday was the first time I picked up your book. I read the whole thing in one day. It gave me a lot of insight into what I am dealing with and I wanted to thank you.

I am currently separated from my family and am allowed to see my kids only two times a week. I have never felt this kind of pressure before and I know that my wife's heart has never been broken like this before. My wife is repulsed by me and does not want me to ever live with them again or ever touch her again. I cannot change the horrible things I have done but I know God can turn them around if I change and obey. I am believing for God to restore all that has been lost.

Tell your men to learn from my mistakes!

Thank you for your ministry,

Michael

What Michael did took guts. Following his confession, he would have to absorb a lot of pain. Most men are not brave enough to face the music, do the hard work of repentance, accept the repercussions, and pursue restoration. Yet, we know there is no such thing as painless growth.

In Michael's case it meant taking on the pain of:

- fully owning the sin
- looking his bride in the eyes and asking her forgiveness
- facing his two little girls—"Daddy blew it and that's why I can't live here any more."
- feeling his life spiraling out of control
- controlling nothing and needing to humbly ask for help
- dealing with public humiliation
- taking on a new label—"adulterer"

The emotions that come with taking on these consequences are unbearable for most men. It doesn't even have to be of a sexual nature to be incredibly difficult. Many bail out of this man-sized responsibility, get defensive, excuse themselves, and accuse others like children. But Michael took a different path. He leapt off the cliff of safety and into the dense fog of confession and repentance. He knew he wouldn't see the sun for a long time, but in his mind the risks were worth it. He wanted to be "healed and used for Christ again."

He leapt off the cliff of safety and into the dense fog of confession and repentance. He knew he wouldn't see the sun for a long time, but in his mind the risks were worth it.

We can all relate to the pain. I've had many a kickback from my own sin. So after praying for Michael at my desk, I wrote him this note:

> Dear Michael,
>
> My heart is breaking with yours and your wife's over this sin. At certain times in my marriage I can easily see myself being right where you are—you are not alone. Your heart is in the right place.

Remember that brokenness comes before blessing. You are broken—soft—moldable—grieving your sin—hating the pain you caused and the feelings they have produced in your wife's heart—and, yet, you are believing that God can take this hell and do something good with it.

How you respond to this will determine your legacy. People will remember how you finished your life versus how you started it. God can bring beauty from ashes and gladness from mourning. You will arise from the ashes a different man as a result of what has happened and God will use it.

Stand on Nahum 1:7 which says, "The LORD is good, a refuge in times of trouble. He cares for those who trust in him." Get some other promises and stand on them with all your soul, strength, and might.

You will make it—one day at a time.

Kenny

Part of the Plan

I think the greatest weakness God's man can have is being unaware of weaknesses. Let me ask you: *What is the most expensive mistake you have ever made?* I'm not talking about losing a deal, buying a lemon at the auto dealer, or purchasing a home that started depreciating the day after you bought it. I am talking about mistakes that cost you in your relationships, took a toll on your physical and spiritual well-being, or exacted a price in your life that you're still paying for today. What comes to mind?

The next question is: *What role have the consequences played in your spiritual journey and service to the Lord?* Every Tuesday morning, my brother Chris teaches a Bible study for men on probation at a rehab center in

Santa Cruz, California. I called him the other day to see how it was going, and he told me about a released felon who told my brother (in different words) where he could take this God stuff and shove it.

Big mistake, I thought, and not just because my brother can bench-press more than three hundred pounds.

Chris paused for a second and then tears mixed with love and righteous anger came flooding out of my brother's mouth as he addressed this guy in front of the class. "You think I'm some rich, white do-gooder here to tell you how to live? That I don't know you? Tell me something, how's your program worked for you so far? Why are you here? Where have you just been? Twenty years ago I was you, sitting in that same chair, thinking and saying the exact same thing. I've seen your movie, and the ending isn't all that great. If you didn't need to be here, you wouldn't be. So sit down, shut your mouth, and listen up, or you'll be out of this program so fast it'll make your head spin. Don't tell me I don't know you. I *am* you!"

You won't see Chris on TV. He is not a celebrity. But he is a hero—my kind of hero.

I smiled at the memory of making the phone call to get Chris into that same program some twenty years ago. Today he's a partner in a financial services company who used some of those great skills God had given him to learn business and finance from the ground up, making a lot of people a lot of money. He's come a long way from where he used to sit—in a court-ordered chair with a bunch of other guys who didn't want to be there. But Jesus needed him to be in that chair so that one day he could come back and have this colorful conversation with a new program member.

You won't see Chris on TV. He is not a celebrity. But he is a hero—my kind of hero. He shares his testimony with those men as freely as he shares the Bible or a cup of coffee with a man who feels the way he once felt—hopeless and ashamed of what he had become. He'll be the first to admit that he's not a polished preacher, but I have never seen anyone more effective with those men. It takes a special guy with a special story and a special past to crack the armor of such hardened hearts.

Big mistake, ***I thought, and not just because my brother can bench-press more than three hundred pounds.***

Most of them hang on every word. Why? 'Cause he's been there. He risks allowing God to use his pains, mistakes, failures, and losses in the past to serve other people. In fact, when you see him in action, you can't help but think that somehow those painful experiences he had to go through in the past were *always* a part of the plan.

Thorny Issues

God has lots of plans for our mistakes and weaknesses. It's counterintuitive to most men to think that way because our style is to hide them. So for a man to accept his failures, losses, and struggles as part of who he is (that is, reality), not things to be hidden away and ignored, is a big leap of faith. It's even more risky to allow God to use those same things to serve other people. Yet that is exactly what my brother did and what Michael did with his letter to me. Remember?

Tell your men to learn from my mistakes!

I began taking Michael's letter with me to conferences around the country because it fit perfectly into one of the sessions called Ready for Reality. In this session I talk to men about how the world won't give us the facts about sin, how men rationalize the facts in order to make space to sin, and how the devil only focuses on your feelings in the moment. Then I say, "But Michael will tell you the facts," and I read his letter. Every time I read this to an audience of men, you can hear a pin drop. All men are convicted by his honesty and candor about his sin, the consequences, the pain, and his belief in God that somehow He will use it all for His glory. When I get to the line about telling the men to learn from his mistakes, I pause. I want them to feel the ministry of truth. It is dead silent, and you can feel the Spirit of Truth breaking through all the rationalizations and justifications for sinning in that very moment. Everyone can sense the power of God coming to them through his brokenness and weakness. The worst of times in a man's life is being used effectively for the Lord. Go figure.

Follow what God's man did after a titanic moral failure in his life:

- He ended the sin.
- He confessed it.
- He accepted full responsibility.
- He grieved over it and the losses it was creating.
- He embraced the reality of who he'd become.
- He allowed God to use it.
- He decided to use it to help others.

And today, tens of thousands of men have been touched by Michael's willingness to let God use the most painful episode in his life.

At times we all wonder why God allows us to experience such incredible pain. There seems to be no point in it. Whether it is something we did or something someone else did to us or something we had no control over, if we are willing to let Him use it, He can bring about His glory through our thorny issues we wish we didn't have to talk about. The best and most effective God's men are the ones who risk talking about their biggest source of shame or biggest obstacle they face as a man. Listen to this letter from another God's man, the apostle Paul:

God's plan is to use the very things we want to keep a secret or keep hidden.

> So I wouldn't get a big head, I was given the gift of a handicap to keep me in constant touch with my limitations. Satan's angel did his best to get me down; what he in fact did was push me to my knees. No danger then of walking around high and mighty! At first I didn't think of it as a gift, and begged God to remove it. Three times I did that, and then he told me,
>
> > My grace is enough; it's all you need.
> > My strength comes into its own in your weakness.
>
> Once I heard that, I was glad to let it happen. I quit focusing on the handicap and began appreciating the gift. It was a case of Christ's strength moving in on my weakness. Now I take limitations in stride, and with good cheer, these limitations that cut me down to size—abuse, accidents, opposition, bad breaks. I just let Christ take over! And so the weaker I get, the stronger I become." (2 Corinthians 12:7–10, MSG)

Paul's little handicap, or "thorn," was a part of his life now. It was always going to be there, and it was a source of struggle and pain. Instead of removing it, God's solution was to:

- keep Paul's pride in check
- display His power through Paul's weakness
- prevent self-sufficiency
- remind Paul of his dependence on God
- expand his ministry to believers
- identify him more deeply with Christ
- deepen his worship
- deemphasize his personal efforts and effectiveness as God's man

God's plan is to use the very things we want to keep a secret or keep hidden. In fact, one of the greatest things he wants to do is to bring us into the truth of reality to encourage others who are struggling with our same issues. "He comes alongside us when we go through hard times, and before you know it, he brings us alongside someone else who is going through hard times so that we can be there for that person just as God was there for us" (2 Corinthians 1:4, MSG). So maybe instead of minimizing or trying to forget your struggles, failures, losses, temptations, or mistakes, let God use them! Instead of praying and asking God to take away your problems or past, ask God to do something with them.

Men have a hard time owning up to their mistakes, much less sharing their shortcomings and hang-ups. Not manly. Exactly—it's not manly, it's godly! It's not about you, your friend's opinions, or what the culture says you should or should not talk about. It's about what God wants to do with the unpleasant parts of your life. He loves the stuff that we would dismiss as unspiritual, ugly, or unsightly and assigns it major importance. More amazingly, He uses those issues to capture ears and hearts.

The best and most effective God's men are the ones who risk talking about their biggest source of shame or biggest obstacle they face as a man.

If I traveled the world and spoke to men about all my achievements and victories, they would be bored out of their minds! They would check out because there is nothing of value when I toot my own horn and emphasize only my strengths. Instead I talk about all my struggles with:

- sexual temptation
- character issues like pride and fear
- my crushing desire to be accepted and the idiotic masks I wore while I chased this elusive status called "cool"
- my lack of a father and that huge loss
- my marriage
- my own imbedded dark side
- working with dying cancer patients
- being honest

All these things are not the yellow brick roads of my life. They are more like the back alleys of my thoughts and life. They are situations where weaknesses or doubts are fought. They are where I fought and lost and got up again to fight another day. They are the places I begged God for help, ran to His Word, and felt His power. I have learned the value of these times like the ancient God's man who wrote in the Psalms, "It was good for me to be afflicted so that I might learn your decrees" (119:71). Times of weakness, struggle, and trial are when we become spiritually rich.

When I switch the focus of my life over to my strengths, accomplishments, achievements, and successes, I am in big trouble. Anytime I hear a man talking in these terms, I know he is in trouble. Anytime I hear a preacher shouting continuously about how God can't be glorified through a testimony that includes struggle and sin, I know God wants to vomit.

If we don't face our struggles, express them to God and other men, and allow them to assist others, we're in serious trouble.

"Don't You Dare!"

You know, Satan hates that we're having this little dialogue about our weaknesses and secrets, our trials and temptations, and our failures and mistakes. He loves when we keep these Achilles heels in the famous "lock box" (à la Al Gore). He knows what's at stake. He knows that without weaknesses, my brother:

- Your temptations will increase.
- You will tend to do things in your own power.
- You will draw attention to you.
- You will be living a lie.
- You will miss out on encouraging others.
- You will not be an effective agent for God's kingdom—especially with other men.

So if you feel conflicted or confused in this discussion, if it is not making sense and you think I am off my spiritual rocker, what you are feeling is not the burger you ate for lunch today. The presence of the Evil One is a constant threat. With all the ways God could use your weaknesses and problems in the lives of others, you can believe the Enemy is going to throw out some major artillery to prevent you from facing those most sensitive areas and insecurities as a man. He wants you to minimize any weaknesses you might have, as though they don't really exist. Then you can get right back to relying on yourself.

A spiritual risk is required to end the shady deal.

- Satan will lie and encourage you to place no faith or trust in God. *"Just give it some time to distance yourself from that, and you'll eventually forget you ever did it."*

  Fact: Time doesn't heal problems and wounds, it only gives them opportunity to grow, hidden and kept in the dark recesses of our characters. When we ignore the truth about who we are and what we deal with, the problem only gets bigger. The truth fades and is replaced by the lie that everything's cool. A spiritual risk is required to end the shady deal.
- Or Satan will appeal to your shame. *"You can't serve God until you have victory over that temptation, overcome that issue, or have been healed of your loss."*

  Fact: Your life will never make sense to you or to the people who know your problems until you let God use the problems, past mistakes, and present struggles to help others. This requires taking a spiritual risk and trusting God.

- Satan will magnify your paranoia or fear of exposure. *"What will people think of you if you share that? What will happen to your image? Don't be a fool!"*

  Fact: God's power and strength will invade your authenticity, and you will become real to those who are fake and dangerous to those looking for safety. Authenticity always leads to credibility (everybody loves someone strong enough to be honest), which leads to vulnerability and trust.

The only course left is to offer God your trust and risk being real.

What's your Achilles heel? Tell someone.

chapter 10

do you have a space invader?

Never go into water alone. Never go into battle alone. Never, ever walk alone. Stay together, Rangers! Live together…and if necessary, die together.

—Stu Weber

On Thanksgiving morning 2003, I woke up at 7:00 a.m. to participate in that cruel rite of manhood fought on the frozen tundra—the Turkey Bowl. I love playing football on Turkey Day and so do about twenty other guys in my community. We know how stupid this ritual is and also that many of us are likely to suffer serious injury. But this year was different because I was in shape! I had been playing in a men's soccer league for the past year and had already pulled every muscle and taken sufficient time to recover. In my mind I was better, stronger, and faster than I had been in a long time.

This illusion of invincibility lasted the entire Turkey Day, all through our vicious touch-football game and well into the very last play, when I zigged and the plantar tendon in my calf zagged. Snap! There was a small explosion under my skin. A few others turned at the sound and saw me crumple to the ground as my brain registered what felt like a Roger Clemens fastball cratering into the back of my leg. I whipped around to find the culprit and saw what looked like a golf ball lodged under the skin of my calf.

Owwuh! Okay, actually the expletive I shouted was a bit more colorful. But it happens on occasion. A mixture of humiliation, self-pity, and incredible pain shot through my veins.

I hobbled off the field and proceeded to spend the next four agonizing days trying to recover on my own. Finally, I swallowed my pride, bit the health-care bullet, and went to a sports orthopedist. When I walked through the door, I was greeted by a museum of sawed-off leg casts hanging like prize game on the walls. Each cast was supposed to represent a person who, like me, had suffered a sports injury and recovered. I checked in, was escorted to an examination room, and waited on the exam bench for the leg doctor.

God's man is never instructed to self-diagnose his own character.

After asking me about the athletic events that had led to the demise of my football career, he stated, "Let's have a look," and proceeded to cup my heel in his left hand while gently squeezing and probing my calf muscle with his right. Then came the words every patient wants to hear: "Okay, Ken, this might hurt a little bit." Before I could respond, he proceeded to drive his thumb into my calf muscle. For those two seconds I could have sworn he was using a red-hot poker to sear through my flesh.

His in-depth medical analysis? "Yep, you ruptured it." *Gee, thanks, Doc.*

"Until you can put pressure on your leg without pain again, you should not participate (insert deliberately slow voice here) *in aaaannnnyyyy sssspppoooorrrrttttssss.*"

As if the past few days weren't painful enough. As if his bill for this little field trip wasn't going to hurt even worse.

Ace bandage: $5.85.

Visit to the orthopedist: $240.

My reaction: Priceless.

I sat there in disbelief, asking God why. *Why did I have to come in to get this looked at?* I knew the answer, but I was angry at the reality. I knew the doctor had told me what I needed to hear. I knew he had told me the truth based on the evidence he'd observed. *I* was the one who'd presented myself to him, not the other way around. And my reaction wasn't relevant to his examination. He was the man I needed to get to the truth and, more important, the man I needed to share it with me. No speculation, no concern about making me uncomfortable. And I was majorly ticked off by it.

I didn't want him examining me, poking around in my most painful spot. But am I glad he did? Absolutely. I had to go to him to know the *real* deal with my leg.

God's man is never instructed to self-diagnose his own character. He's not asked to make self-assessments or draw personal conclusions about his own condition. We don't have the training, objectivity, or perspective to see the facts about ourselves, spiritually or relationally. We all have blind spots that only someone on the outside is positioned to point out. God's role is private. Going "public" with another man is more of a stretch for us. It's risky. We have to trust that God knows this when He tells us to seek out and find a space invader.

Getting Examined

Sometimes it's risky to present ourselves for examination, because we know what it will involve. That's why men are notorious for trying to shake off injuries, playing hurt, coming back too early, and not getting stuff checked out by a real physician. Deep down we don't want to hear, "You are going to have to stop playing." *No! Not gonna do it!* Instead, we want to gut it out, wrap it up, put some ice on it, get a knee brace, just ignore the pain. We are either too prideful or too scared or both. If we neglect or ignore it, we suffer. But if we neglect our character by not getting it examined by another godly man, people and the kingdom of God suffer.

I was afraid, very, very afraid for people to know the dark side, the struggling side, and the wounds in my character.

We need to remember: accountability is not about us. My friend Stu Weber has reframed ambitious accountability for me. In his book *All the King's Men* (yes, this is a personal plug), Stu exposes our excuses against pursuing a spiritual space invader and replaces them with the true necessity of a knowing brother.

> The thrust of Accountability is not meant to be punitive, but preventive. It's not to yell after your brother as he plummets over the

> cliff, "See what you get, you jerk?" It's to say, "I'm committed to your good. When you need me, I'll act as a human guardrail for you. I'm not made of steel, but I cannot watch you go over the cliff without warning you. And I want to warn you right at the road's edge where you still have an opportunity to regain control."[1]

Fellowship with other men will get you only so far. I know lots of guys in men's groups who are still the same guys with the same character producing the same problems year after year. They haven't narrowed their group down to one or two men and *expressed* the need for the next level of accountability to them—the kind that has teeth that bite hard and leave a mark. Listen to King David describe his desire to please God and his need for space invaders—guys close enough to knock him on his can! "Let a righteous man strike me—it is a kindness; let him rebuke me—it is oil on my head. My head will not refuse it" (Psalm 141:5). David knew he needed a real male friend, not a fan.

David knew he needed a real male friend, not a fan.

The margin of victory for most men is one other man—a strong, caring space invader. I can't believe how long I was a Christian and never once encountered a man who cared enough to get in my space over obvious issues. Maybe the Christians I hung around with didn't feel I needed to be shaken down. As a consequence, I was winning the battle of images and masks while losing the war for character and Christlikeness. Part of it was definitely me. I was afraid, very, very afraid for people to know the dark side, the struggling side, and the wounds in my character. Letting someone see under my body armor might mean bugged-out eyeballs and deep gasping for air. But the other part of it was the men in my life who did not know what real accountability looked like and who, too, were afraid of showing their sores for the sake of Christ.

The most frustrating aspect of this kind of existence is that we are not progressing. Instead of becoming the men we need to be, we're remaining who we are. In not seeking a space invader, I was failing on the most important spiritual battle front—my character. Most Christian men are unexamined, unknown, unconfessed, and unable to risk transparency for the sake of growth. It's tough to watch men—especially leaders—whose influence exceeds their unchecked character issues. God has to bench them, retrain them, and rebuild them. It calls to mind Howard Hendricks's study of 246 pastors who lost their ministries because of affairs.[2] The four common denominators in the lives of these men:

1. Their devotional lives became stale or academic.
2. They had no accountability.
3. They thought it was okay to counsel women alone.
4. They thought it could never happen to them.

No one was asking these leaders:

- "How's your soul?"
- "Did you spend time with Jesus? What did you do?"
- "Are you loving your wife?"
- "Are you seeking her best?"
- "Have you fought with her this week? Why?"
- "Have you been emotionally tempted this week?"
- "Are you disciplining your eyes sexually?"
- "Have you been alone with a woman not your wife?"
- "Have you spent time with your kids?"

- "Are you responsible for your success, or is God?"
- "Is your pride out of whack?"

That's why all of us need to get over the fear of being known. We need to take a step of faith and embrace *aggressive* accountability before it's too late. If we don't, we will plateau in our growth as leaders or, worse, become blind in our pride and destroy ourselves. The biting reality is that there is no neutral gear when it comes to accountability. You have to be moving forward in Christlikeness and making new choices in your conduct as a result.

Are you getting looked at regularly by at least one other man who doesn't care about your image, doesn't read your press clippings, and doesn't buy your spin? This man who cares about you becoming God's man needs full permission to examine, press, and push. He has an eye for Christlikeness and a sniper's rifle trained on your pride.

Symbiotic Accountability

Spiritual independence is an oxymoron. The key word here is *moron.*

"My relationship with God is personal" is a common refrain. I hear this from men who don't have the spine to accept responsibility or to admit a fault, or both. Saying it to a men's pastor is the verbal equivalent of a skunk facing south with its tail raised: it's code for "Get on your bike and pedal, or else." There are lots of reasons men respond this way. Shame, selfishness, ignorance, wounds, and defects produced by a sinful nature are the major culprits. But for the man who has experienced the slimy pits of self-sufficiency, who has been broken by his sin and awakened by grace, and has tasted God's goodness, this reaction is worse than counterproductive. It invites God's discipline.

God's man is designed to live interdependently with another brother. This accountability is a locking of arms that grows stronger over time. The myth is that deep spiritual maturity should require less accountability over time. It certainly sounds good. But those 246 pastors would probably tell you the opposite is true.

This "symbiotic accountability" is highlighted in Paul's exhortation to the Thessalonian church. Reconnaissance by Paul's protégé Timothy showed good spiritual progress, and his reports were off the charts. Their report card according to 1 Thessalonians 3:6–9 was:

- Faith A+
- Love A+
- Commitment A+

What do you say to disciples like these? Listen closely to how Paul managed the news and responded to the men in Thessalonica who might have been feeling as if they had the Jesus thing wired.

> Finally, brothers, we instructed you how to live in order to please God, as in fact you are living. Now we ask you and urge you in the Lord Jesus to do this more and more. For you know what instructions we gave you by the authority of the Lord Jesus.
>
> It is God's will that you should be sanctified: that you should avoid sexual immorality; that each of you should learn to control his own body in a way that is holy and honorable, not in passionate lust like the heathen, who do not know God; and that in this matter no one should wrong his brother or take advantage of him. The Lord will punish men for all such sins, as we have already told you and warned you. (1 Thessalonians 4:1–6)

Red alert! Warning! Personal space being invaded!

The message from Paul to the men of Thessalonica was unmistakable:

- "I affirm you and your progress to this point."
- "I am not letting you stay comfortable."
- "I am focused on the next area of spiritual integrity."
- "I am in your spiritual life to stretch you."
- "I am going to invade your space in Jesus's name."
- "I am asking and urging you to keep stretching spiritually."
- "I see an area you need to work on—keep your togas down!"
- "I am going to call it like I see it."
- "I do not need an invitation or a crisis to speak up."

If I were a Thessalonian believer, I might push back and get in Paul's face. "What authority do you have to get into my business? Isn't that between me and the Lord?" Paul knows this, and that is why he says, "We ask you, we urge you in the Lord Jesus...by the authority of the Lord Jesus." In other words, "In the Lord Jesus, *your* business *is* my business and *my* business is your business."

Brother to brother, believer to believer, we are deputized by Jesus and given the authority in Him to firmly and gently encourage a brother to line his life up with his identity and responsibility as God's man. It's not about the messenger, his character, or even his delivery. It's about who he represents, the truthfulness of his observation, and his faithfulness to God's purpose for the relationship.

What is the relationship between a clown fish and a sea anemone? Lobbyists and political parties? Abbott and Costello? Dean Martin and Jerry

Lewis? All these relationships are symbiotic. Symbiosis is the connectedness of two dissimilar organisms or people that is mutually beneficial. What about God's men in a local body of believers, a house church, a small group? Rob and Darren. Bill and Howard. Scott and Dave. Mike and Frank. Two dissimilar men who have unique skills, passions, natural abilities, personalities, and life experiences, mysteriously connected by God and mutually benefiting. Designed differently, but put together for a specific kingdom purpose by the Creator.

In other words, "In the Lord Jesus, your business is my business and my business is your business."

So what? What's actually at stake if you don't enter that kind of spiritual relationship with another man or two? The less accountable God's men are, the sicker the body becomes, because it has got undetected cancers of character growing. The more accountable we are as God's men, the healthier we are as individuals, and consequently, the healthier the body of believers becomes. That's why more of God's men need to have a Jonathan and David moment. One God's man simply commits to the other that "The LORD is witness between you and me" (1 Samuel 20:42). In other words, we are each other's spiritual space invaders; we won't let each other fail spiritually.

Solomon saw clearly that our spiritual direction is determined by our willingness to be deeply connected and accountable to men of character. He instructs, "Thus you will walk in the ways of good men and keep to the paths of the righteous" (Proverbs 2:20). We are better together, but that means taking a purposeful risk.

As a spiritual mechanic, I always check a man's relationships with other men first. That's the oil of spiritual growth in a man's life and the quickest way to get a reading. If he's down a quart or two on accountability, his spiritual engine is working harder to get the same performance, running hotter, and dealing with sludge in moving parts. The most damaging effect is to his relationships. I hammer away at men to make sure they are connected to at least one man who has permission to invade their space.

What about you? Are you battling low spiritual performance? Who are the men around you?

Your spiritual direction isn't the only thing determined by the invaders of your space. There's also your spiritual finish. Listen to the writer of Hebrews push his men. "We want each of you to show this same diligence to the very end, in order to make your hope sure. We do not want you to become lazy, but to imitate those who through faith and patience inherit what has been promised" (Hebrews 6:11–12). I imagine the writer had the same twisted DNA as my basketball coach in high school. He would make us run drills at the end of every practice. We were all exhausted, and he would shout the dreaded statement: "Everybody on the line!" We'd moan and whine, knowing we would be pushed past fatigue beyond the three hours of pushing ourselves in practice. To make a good team great, a coach has to condition you and stretch your limits to get familiar with that kind of struggle. No one complained about the drills when we won twenty-two out of twenty-three games that season including the league championship. Space invaders make good men great.

Want to finish strong spiritually? Get a space invader.

The Beach Landing

So what's the process of finding a space invader and landing in each others' lives? How should it feel? To what areas do you give access? What does aggressive accountability look like? We can take our cue from one of the best space invaders who ever lived. Paul writes:

> We *proclaim* Him, *admonishing* every man and *teaching* every man with all wisdom, so that we may *present* every man *complete* in Christ. For this purpose also I labor, striving according to His power, which mightily works within me." (Colossians 1:28–29, NASB, emphasis added)

When I have been placed by God in community with another man for the purposes of spiritual growth and have his permission and willingness to be accountable, I need to emphasize those same five things.

1. *Proclamation.* Space invasion is an outreach. Beneath it all, an accountability relationship expresses a commitment to God and His will. The foundation from which advice is given, problems are resolved, and issues are settled is Jesus Christ. "Whatever you do, whether in word or deed, do it all in the name of the Lord Jesus, giving thanks to God the Father through him" (Colossians 3:17). We are reaching out to a brother in Jesus's name and for His sake, not our own, putting Christ front and center.
2. *Admonition.* Space invasion is filled with gentle yet firm warnings against evil. When there is a moral, sexual, relational, financial, or spiritual temptation, we come out strongly, convicting from God's Word. We don't have to be loud; God's Word will do the shouting

for us. We are simply to patrol and watch the bushes for Enemy movement, doing spiritual warfare together.

3. *Education.* Class is always in session with your space invader. The relationship is all about learning and growing with another man. Each man has unique strengths and weaknesses, and when we share and receive those "in all wisdom," we become stronger God's men. Jesus said God's man is to be about the business of "teaching them to obey everything I have commanded you" for as long as we've got a pulse (Matthew 28:20). Whatever insight, wisdom, and spiritual gifts we are given from God are to be shared as well as received from others. We are to teach *and* learn from each other.
4. *Presentation.* Space invasion is all about pushing a man to *live out* his values. In a sense, Paul says that he puts his "spiritual investments" (specifically, other men) on display. He says that proclamation, admonition, and education go into the presentation of every man. The guys close to him are proudly displayed as men of character. Each of them reflects the time, effort, and personal training he has put into them for Christ. That is why a space invader needs to push hard for spiritual integrity, being undivided between what men believe and how they really live and think. Every man the space invader touches is a walking billboard of his efforts. You will invest whatever is necessary not to let him fail on your watch.
5. *Completion.* Space invasion encompasses *every domain* of a man's relationship with God and others. The end game is full maturity, "completeness in Christ." We want that man to be mature, lacking nothing in his moral, marital, spiritual, and family life. We seek the full development of God's purposes by watching his connection to other men in fellowship. We ask specific questions about his discipleship, his worship, his service, and his evangelism. Is he spending time

with Jesus through prayer, confession, and Scripture? How is his heart for and love of Jesus? Is he developing his spiritual gifts and using them to minister to other believers? Is he seeking out opportunities to tell someone else what Christ has done in his life?

In the process of discovering all these things, we will experience:

- mentoring like Elijah and Elisha in 1 and 2 Kings
- truth-telling like David and Nathan in 1 Samuel
- strength under great pressure like Daniel and his friends in ancient Babylon
- intense healing of personal defects like Naaman and Elijah in 2 Kings
- the excitement of new frontiers of blessing like Joshua and Caleb
- coming through the storms together like Jesus and His disciples
- serious confrontation like Jesus's difficult words to Peter about his love for Him
- life lived for an audience of One as Paul encouraged Timothy
- a bold witness like Peter and John
- the achievement of co-labor for God's kingdom like Nehemiah and Ezra
- the dynamic expansion of ministry as other men join in fellowship like Solomon and David in 1 Chronicles 28–29

These are great feats for God accomplished by great men through the power of intimate community.

So the big questions are: *Are you ready to invade? Are you willing to be invaded?*

chapter 11

the ruthless way

May God have mercy upon my enemies, because I won't.

—General George S. Patton Jr.

On February 8, 2005, Brian "Head" Welch dropped a letter in the mail to his band. He was resigning as lead guitarist. It happens all the time in the music industry. But this particular decision of defection was not over a feud about money, ambition, or power. The band that opened this little note from Brian was multiplatinum-selling Korn, with over eleven million records sold.

Nope, it wasn't about the buck. This was about holiness.

"Head" was on the warpath in his walk with God. More specifically, he was setting out to exterminate sin from every beachhead of his life. There would be no accommodation and no mercy shown.

According to Chad Bonham, who chronicled Welch's merciless pursuit of holiness in *New Man* magazine, Brian's "Dear Korn" letter was just the beginning.

> He removed the platinum records from his wall and replaced them with Scripture posters. He cleaned the drug stash out of his closet and turned it into a prayer sanctuary. Welch is also very candid about his past struggles with sexual addiction and self-gratification, a problem for which he found a rather unique solution.
>
> "It says in the Bible, if your right hand causes you to sin, cut it off," Welch says. "I was addicted to porn, so I cut my right hand off by putting 'J.E.S.U.S.' on my knuckles. I got 'J.E.S.U.S' tattooed on my knuckles, and people laugh about that. Just yesterday my left hand caused me to sin, so I got 'M.A.R.K. 9:43' tattooed on my other hand."[1]

Mark 9:43 says, "If your hand causes you to sin, cut it off. It is better for you to enter life maimed than with two hands to go into hell, where the fire never goes out." All I have to say about Welch's method is "Whoa!" Brian is ruthless exactly because he is God's man. For now, his taste of salvation has altered his taste for sin. Self-indulgence has been replaced with self-sacrifice. Behavioral tendencies are being aggressively replaced with behavioral responsibilities as God's man. He is breaking the ties that bind him to the old man with a holy viciousness reserved only for those inclinations and actions that might attack his relationship with his Savior and harm his relationship with God and people. His interpretation of Jesus's instruction regarding personal sin areas in Mark 9 is right on the money—be merciless.

> ***"I was addicted to porn, so I cut my right hand off by putting 'J.E.S.U.S' on my knuckles."***

Tariq (*Tar*-ick) Seifullah has the right idea too. I connected with him at an Every Man Conference in Columbus, Ohio. You could say he was hard to miss. I'd gotten to my point about "picking a fight" with sin. All of a sudden, a couple of rows back, I saw this young man with braided hair stand up in front of three hundred other men. He sprang up, threw a few air punches, and roared "Come on now!" To be honest, it caught me off guard. But I instinctively knew why Tariq was up and out of seat—his warlike soul had been tapped.

We talked afterward, and he told me that he was tired of sin, tired of compromise, and tired of losing. He told me he stood up because he hated giving in to sin and it was time for a radical new mentality—eradication. With his new direction, Tariq was ready to take no prisoners. A week later I got this in my inbox.

> Dear Kenny,
>
> I am Tariq and you told me to keep in touch with you. I must personally say that I have been walking victoriously since the Every Man Conference last weekend. I have been more transparent, turning my head during beer commercials of football games [ha-ha], and doing the little things has made my personal battle against sin much easier. I am "training instead of trying" that I might be a champ not a chump for Christ. Doing the simple things repetitively has been improving my walk with Christ greatly!
>
> I am heading to DC for a White House internship. I ask that you keep me in your prayers that I may stand like Daniel and Joseph, that I may receive the boldness of David, the wisdom of Solomon, and the faith of Abraham. God must be first in my life. I will need accountability and prayer. Thank you so much for coming to our church.
>
> In Him,
>
> Tariq

Both Brian and Tariq have made a power shift in their souls. They have stopped shaking hands with sin like an old friend, as if they're old buddies, and in the words of the Puritan preacher Benjamin Needler, have "shaken it off like a viper into the fire." To these warriors, sin is not something to manage, it is something to destroy. They have recognized it as the enemy of their spiritual freedom.

"I am 'training instead of trying' that I might be a champ not a chump for Christ."

> We have an obligation—but it is not to the sinful nature, to live according to it. For if you live according to the sinful nature, you will die; but if by the Spirit you *put to death* the misdeeds of the body, you will live, because those who are led by the Spirit of God are sons of God. (Romans 8:12–14, emphasis added)

To be God's man means to hate indwelling sin with a passion.

Clean Out the Closets

The part of Brian's story that speaks loudest to me was the cleaning out of his closets. He boldly and intentionally went after his drug stashes, which he looked upon as roadside bombs for his new identity as God's man. He was sending a clear message to the old Brian that the breakup would be final and every last visible remnant would be dealt with forcefully. It started with his friendships (in leaving the band), extending to the idols (the platinum records on the wall), and then on to the substitutes for real intimacy (drugs and sex).

I remember going through this same process with my brother after praying to receive Christ in my kitchen at 3:00 a.m. back in 1982. We scoured my closets and found all kinds of baddies from *Playboy* magazines to dirty word Scrabble! But the reason Brian's pursuit intrigued me was that, though I'd cleaned out the closets of my house, the real war was with the closets of my character. Those invisible affections, stealth desires, concealed weapons, unseen temptations, and hidden pride no one could see but me and God. *That* is the battle I am still on, hunting down those strongholds in my character with God's help.

In some ways, this battle against indwelling sin resembles the complexities of the War on Terror. First of all, intelligence is critical. The Enemy is shifty, hidden, networked, armed, and patient, and he knows you are after him. He can employ disguises, disinformation, and poisonous deception to keep you at bay. He has powerful allies (namely, the media-soaked culture and the devil) supplying him with ammunition. He knows when you sleep and when you wake up.

How do you find rest from this war on spiritual terror? Once you have cut off the snake's head, it grows another somewhere else just as lethal. J. I. Packer puts it this way, "Sin is always at work in the heart; a temporary lull in its assaults means not that it is dead, but that it is very much alive."

What roadside bombs are stowed away in your closets today? An Every Man Ministries poll reveals the predominant masculine sins that need to be constantly tracked down reside in one or more of the following areas. Do your checklist, and I'll do mine.

- lust or fantasy sex
- pride

- unresolved marital disconnection or infidelity
- materialism
- anger or resentments
- busyness or workaholism
- unforgiveness
- selfishness
- jealousy or envy
- impatience
- comparison
- spiritual apathy

These are some terrorists sponsored by sin and living on our own soil that seek to sabotage our relationships with God and people. They are relentless and crafty character qualities that camp in caves and hide. But we can't let them get a peaceful night's rest. We must search them out and find ways to disable and dismantle their network with our powerful, God-given tools.

Here's how to perform "exploratory surgery":

1. *We ask God to reveal sin directly to us.* This simply means inviting God to explore the landscapes of our lives and relationships in order to reveal to us those actions and attitudes we need to deal with directly. We say with David, "Search me, O God, and know my heart; test me and know my anxious thoughts. See if there is any offensive way in me, and lead me in the way everlasting" (Psalm 139:23–24). First we give God the freedom to search us and open up any closet He wants. Second, we invite testing to reveal our true character. Third, we ask for conviction of anything displeasing to Him. Fourth, we ask for His guidance out of sinful patterns over to clean ones that are right with Him.

2. *We place ourselves under the microscope of Scripture.* Scripture is like spiritual radiation treatment to kill the cancerous cells of sin. Like patients, we must submit to it and accept any loss. It may be friends rather than hair, or an unhealthy attitude instead of weight. It may mean exchanging our mental diet of junk to healthy spiritual fiber. God's Word can snuff out any lingering sin, but God's man must be prepared in advance to accept some personal casualties. By believing in the process of applying Scripture to eliminate the visible sin and weaken the disposition of indwelling sin, God frees us. "I will walk about in freedom, for I have sought out your precepts" (Psalm 119:45).

> ***Scripture is like spiritual radiation treatment to kill the cancerous cells of sin. Like patients, we must submit to it and accept any loss.***

3. *We allow other God's men to freely use the microscope.* While only some of us will get bald spots, we all have blind spots: areas of our lives that we simply can't see or don't want to see or that seem benign to us. But they may in fact be poisonous to us or others. The ruthless way involves empowering space invaders to help root out sin with the authority of Scripture. "It is better to heed a wise man's rebuke than to listen to the song of fools" (Ecclesiastes 7:5).
4. *We ask our wives to be forward observers in our lives.* If you are married, your wife is uniquely positioned to be an intimate ally in the battle against sin in your life. She can provide a voice that warns and protects against any sin she might see developing in you. I know you might be reading this saying, "This guy's nuts. My sins? What about hers?" Don't get defensive. Consider this: *God* gave your wife her role to speak into your life. If God is speaking to her, you have the responsibility to invite her into your growth. Why? Because you

need her! "Her husband has full confidence in her and lacks nothing of value. She brings him good, not harm, all the days of her life" (Proverbs 31:11–12). The question is: Have you given her permission to point out anything inconsistent with God's Word? *That's* the ruthless way!

5. *We kill sin by the piercing vision of the Holy Spirit.* First, the Holy Spirit makes us aware of the sins that need to be eliminated. He will let you, as God's man, clearly know whether something isn't right under the hood. It could be a repeated thought, a sense of unease, a circumstance that confirms a suspicion, or even an undeniable "Aha!" moment as you're reading Scripture. The Holy Spirit living inside you makes that urging possible. Without it, the change either doesn't happen or doesn't happen right. He alone brings Christ's sin-destroying power to move us to freely serve Him. "The Lord is the Spirit, and where the Spirit of the Lord is, there is freedom" (2 Corinthians 3:17). This is why we must learn to recognize His voice, obey it promptly, and invite Him to daily direct and redirect our minds and hearts. Do you have the Holy Spirit in your battle against sin today?

A Clear and Present Danger

In 1656, the Puritan theologian John Owen penned a work called "Of the Mortification of Sin in Believers." Over three hundred years ago he was talking about the very clear and present danger sin poses to our walk with Christ.

> While danger concerns what is future, evil concerns what exists in the present. Presently, sin grieves the Holy Spirit. And we are exhorted to "grieve not the Spirit of God, whereby ye are sealed unto the day of redemption" (Eph. 4:30). If by our ingratitude, we grieve a tender

> and loving friend, what more is it to grieve the tender, loving Spirit of God who has chosen our hearts as His dwelling place?…
>
> Moreover, the Lord Jesus Christ is wounded afresh by the evil of sin. His love is foiled. His enemy is gratified. To harbor sin is to "crucify the Son of God afresh, and put Him to an open shame" (Heb. 6:6).
>
> The evil of sin also takes away a man's usefulness in his generation. His works, his endeavors, his labors seldom receive blessing from God.…
>
> Sin saps a person's obedience to God like a worm at the roots of a plant. Sin deters all the graces of God. How vital it is for us to keep alive the considerations of the guilt, the danger, and the evil of sin. Dwell on their seriousness. Make them a powerful reality in your soul.[2]

You can't read that and not feel convicted! Our sins were not forgiven so that we may casually and contentedly continue in them. Viewing sin seriously, seeking freedom from its bondage, and vigilantly dealing with it is the ongoing preoccupation of God's man. If we aren't dutiful to kill sin, we're abusers of God's grace, which incidentally did not come cheap. Becoming good at tracking sin down is a key message of the Scriptures. "I write this to you so that you will not sin" (1 John 2:1). Elimination is the goal. But John isn't after perfection by our human efforts. "But if anybody does sin, we have one who speaks to the Father in our defense—Jesus Christ, the Righteous One. He is the atoning sacrifice for our sins, and not only for ours but

The evil of sin also takes away a man's usefulness in his present generation. His works, his endeavors, his labors seldom receive blessing from God.

also for the sins of the whole world" (1 John 2:1–2). Beating sin is a lifelong process because we are fallible humans. But John's reminder of Christ's sacrifice recalls the high price, raises our intensity level, and renews our commitment to go after sin with the same passion our King did on that ugly Friday almost two thousand years ago.

Ruthlessness is a term usually reserved for tyrants and insecure dictators. The Hitlers or Husseins of history. Yet, spiritually speaking, there is a tyrant who lives inside of us all that must be spared no mercy. He is not to be managed. He is to be eliminated by our cooperation with God's Spirit on a daily basis. The irony of our spiritual mission is that it is a lifelong pursuit requiring a persistent determination.

There is no complete elimination of sin for the believer on earth. Though the Bible is crystal clear that there is to be a steady weakening of sin through our constant fight, with increasing evidence of frequent success, the final victory will go to the Savior. Through His indwelling power, we can be assured that every effort expended will be rewarded. Without apology, we take any necessary action in our lives and relationships to cause sin to appear as it really is, even if it means:

- new relationships
- new disciplines
- new accountability
- new boundaries
- new appreciation for grace
- new weapons
- new lifestyle
- new mentality
- new determination

- new subscriptions
- new Web filter
- new counselor
- new tattoos
- new Spirit
- new ________________ (fill in the blank)

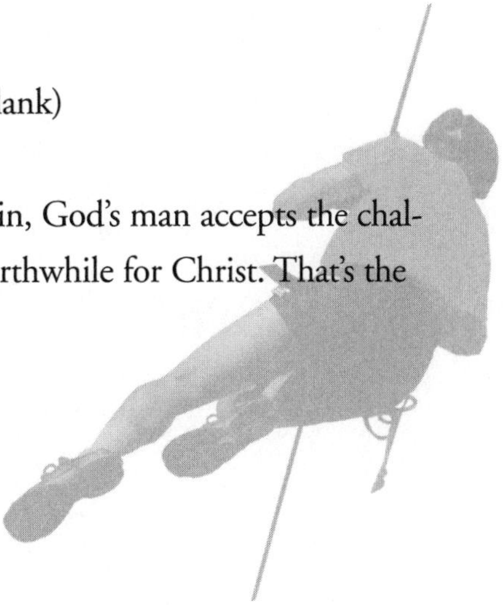

When it comes to ruthlessly eradicating sin, God's man accepts the challenge. If it hurts in the short term, it's worthwhile for Christ. That's the ruthless way.

Cut it out. Get it all. It's the *only* way.

chapter 12

the highest vision, the noblest goal

When the risen Christ is central, you know what is peripheral. Never confuse the two.

—STUART BRISCOE

Ali Malaekeh was charmed from the start. As son of the ambassador to Bulgaria for the Shah and the Iranian government, he enjoyed the benefits of his father's position. Ali and his older brother grew up going to the best schools, joining the best athletic clubs, and living in a beautiful home.

Now imagine being Ali the day your dad comes to explain that this life your family has always known will never be the same. With the rise of Ayatolla Khomeini and the Iranian revolution, the Malaekehs were transformed from public servants into public enemies. When the Shah's regime fell in 1979, Ali's family became fugitives and targets for assassination. His family would have to move to Austria to receive political asylum. Ali could never go home again.

His family moved around to Italy, London, and Vienna for the rest of his adolescence. During that time he developed a budding romance with European football (soccer). Like millions of other European youth, he idolized clubs like AC Milan and Roma, as well as players from Italy like Bruno Conti. He played for his prep school, committing almost every World Cup to memory, and eventually coming to the States to play collegiate soccer. At college, soccer and partying became Ali's religion, and his cultural Muslim roots faded into a distant memory. For certain, Ali was focused. But not on God.

His soccer career progressed from playing to coaching. He landed Division I collegiate assignments, as well as club coaching assignments in Indiana and Kentucky. Eventually he accepted an opportunity in California, coaching the team my daughter Cara was playing for, and that's where our paths crossed.

I was impressed with Ali from the start. He was uncommonly focused and disciplined with the girls. I had no idea where Ali stood spiritually, but I liked him, and I was impelled to assist him any way I could. So I engaged him, brought him some books, and began to pray for him. For some reason, he began to confide in me. All along I was praying and asking God for a chance to introduce Christ into his Muslim background. As I prayed, Ali continued enjoying both his new soccer assignment and the Southern California nightlife.

Around the time Ali's first season was coming to a close, I was at home, working on my computer. My instant-message bell went off. The message was from Ali: "Hi there…do you have a sec?"

I responded, and after a few volleys, Ali said he was looking to change jobs yet again, and he was uncertain about what the future held for him. I could see his dissatisfaction and instantly knew where the conversation was headed. Here was a clear invitation to share Christ, served up on a titanic silver platter!

My reply to Ali was quick and simple: "I don't know if you are a praying man, but I believe God has you out in California for a purpose."

Before I sent it, I paused and asked God to use it as He would. I had no clue how Ali would react *(Lord, I think he's Muslim!).*

In faith, I sent it, and almost immediately, the instant-message window indicated: "Ali is typing."

Okay, Lord, I thought, *here we go. Is he going to rip into me?*

A message popped up: "I strongly agree. God did bring me here for a reason."

Ali proceeded to share that he was searching for a conversation with God. I took a deep breath and told him my story of coming to Christ, encouraging him, if he was feeling the same, to pray a prayer of introduction and invite Christ into his life. I typed out the prayer word for word and told him I would bring a Bible and a few books to the next practice.

Ali sent a reply: "There is so much I would like to share with you and so much I need to learn. I will take your suggestion to heart and pray for an introduction to Christ."

I jumped up, howling at my computer screen and running around the office at Every Man, enlisting anyone with a pulse to pray for Ali's salvation.

Ali stayed in California. During the next year, he and two other soccer coaches committed their lives to Christ and began meeting with me on Tuesday mornings to learn what it means to be God's man and how to share Christ with others. Ali's focus and commitment were truly supernatural. In fact, almost one year later, Ali, a man to whom Ali had witnessed, and I gave our testimonies of God's amazing tapestry of salvation which had mysteriously woven itself around the three of us. I wept as Ali shared in front of almost twenty thousand people over the two-day event. And you could hear a pin drop as he shared. Ali's uncommon focus and determination to be a disciple shines through this excerpt from his testimony.

> I had no idea Kenny was a pastor. If I had known that, given my lifestyle and being raised in a Muslim culture, I would have never asked for his advice. Kenny told me that Jesus wanted me on his team. So now I play on God's team and Jesus is my coach. I live my life so I can please Him. My responsibility is to do what He tells me to do. If I trip and fall, He is there to pick me up. I can turn to my teammates for support and count on them to encourage me in my journey with Christ. How awesome it is to play for a team that I know is going to win! I look forward to the day when my coach is going to lovingly put His arm around me and say, "Well done."

> I shared my faith with all my friends and they laughed at me. They could not believe the changes in my life. They thought I must be going through a phase. One friend, however, was interested. Tony and I had many conversations after practices and I prayed that he too would come to know Jesus. One month after I came to Christ, I invited Tony to start attending Saddleback with me. Surprisingly Tony told me he wanted to go with me to the membership class and to my baptism. At the class, they give an invitation to receive Christ. I looked over and Tony's head was bowed and eyes closed...he turned to me and whispered, "I did it. I just accepted Jesus!" I almost fell out of my chair. Kenny baptized both of us that night.

When I reflect on Ali, his journey, his commitment to Christ, and his laserlike focus on the prize, I am so proud of him. His "goal" orientation from soccer was transplanted right into his journey with God. He fits the sentiments of the famous Dallas, Texas, pastor Dr. Tony Evans, who says, "We don't need more Christians, we've got plenty of Christians. We need more disciples." If you know Dr. Evans, you know he is not questioning the need to evangelize as much as he is commenting on spiritual apathy and the unwillingness to sacrifice comfort for commitment to Christ.

Ali is a disciple and an inspiration to me and all the men of Saddleback. Why? Because he is single-minded about loving God (worship), loving others (service), reaching others (sharing his faith), connecting with other believers (fellowship), and becoming like Christ (discipleship). He has a huge commitment to the Great Commission (Matthew 28:18–20) and the Greatest Commandment (Matthew 22:37–38). This is his life mission, his highest vision, his noblest goal, and the worst the Enemy can dish out will not prevail, as Jesus promised in Matthew 16:18–19. Ali's got it.

As I was writing this chapter, I got a note from Ali updating me on his journey. (He had no idea I was writing about him here; in other words, I didn't ask him to share this):

> Kenny,
>
> I started thinking about all that we spoke about today and in the last twenty months. You used an amazing analogy some two years ago when you told me Jesus wanted me on his team. What a privilege that He would want me on His team. I look at it a bit differently now.
>
> It is still a team but I look at it as a band of brothers going to war. And just like every freshly enlisted Marine who joins to fight, I didn't think I needed basic training. I thought I could go out there, without training, and fight a good fight. Looking back, I thank you for slowing me down. I would have probably caused a lot of casualties and gotten myself killed. But I feel basic training is over. It is time to be deployed. I know I don't have the training of a SEAL or Ranger but I am ready for battle.
>
> There are millions of people out there who need to hear about Jesus's perfect love for us. Innocent children born in areas where the Enemy has a foothold, drug addicts, dealers, prostitutes, and inmates...these people are not experiencing Jesus's power and love. They need to get to know Him. They need to know that there is a path to freedom and it is Jesus.
>
> I am taking up my shield of faith, my helmet of salvation, and the sword of the Spirit and hitting the battlefield. I am going to wait for orders but I am not going to sit down passively. I am going to call on God to send me, to use me because living my life for my sake has no worth to me. From Compton to Jakarta, from London to Johannesburg, I am at His service.

Jesus's precious blood was shed for all of humanity. I can't sit back any longer knowing people are living and dying without Jesus. I have nothing to lose and everything to gain knowing that I have Him in my corner.

In His grasp,

Ali

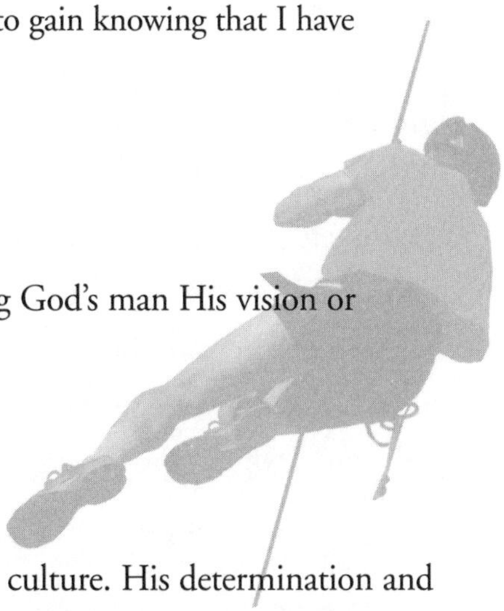

What about you? Is your vision for being God's man His vision or yours?

One Ambition

Ali is an anomaly in today's postmodern culture. His determination and faith fly in the face of a culture that makes feelings and personal beliefs the only true indicators of right and wrong. Today only bigots, terrorists, or political extremists hold to strong beliefs. But that's exactly why Ali will thrive in this age and will be successful wherever he lands. His ambition, focus, and single-minded faith in the Great Commission and the Greatest Commandment come from a grace awakening, not a brainwashing. I want him to stay strong in grace because what saved him will also sustain him as he embarks on a pathway of leadership and service to God.

There is a long tradition of God's leaders encouraging God's men to live out God's purposes single-mindedly. Jesus told His men of His upcoming suffering at the cross and then used that reality to motivate them. He was honest and clear. His men would have to reject other pursuits, carry the responsibility of a God's man, and follow Him loyally to the end. He modeled for us how to call men to a mission. The call to the multitudes was different than the charge to His men.

> Then Jesus said to his disciples, "If anyone would come after me, he must deny himself and take up his cross and follow me." (Matthew 16:24)

Paul's style and approach was equally bold with Timothy in his charge, going so far as to illustrate single-mindedness in three different ways. Read the following as Timothy might have, receiving a scroll from a prison cell in Rome to you in ancient Greece. This will be your last communication from the man who led you to Christ, who trained you in the field, and who now awaits his execution. You read the first part of the note, which conveys encouragement to be faithful, and then you read:

> You then, my son, be strong in the grace that is in Christ Jesus. And the things you have heard me say in the presence of many witnesses entrust to reliable men who will also be qualified to teach others. Endure hardship with us like a good soldier of Christ Jesus. No one serving as a soldier gets involved in civilian affairs—he wants to please his commanding officer. Similarly, if anyone competes as an athlete, he does not receive the victor's crown unless he competes according to the rules. The hardworking farmer should be the first to receive a share of the crops. Reflect on what I am saying, for the Lord will give you insight into all this." (2 Timothy 2:1–7)

Paul knew he had just dropped a bomb on Timothy that would require some heavy reflection. "Pause," he advised. "Think deeply and continuously on what I just said. This is a biggie." Timothy was going to have to take on a single identity, passion, and goal. He would have to train hard, work hard, and focus on results. The examples of commitment Paul meant were not weak wafflers. They were strong men with strong inner convictions who were willing to forgo comfort and discipline themselves to get results consistent with their identities. Paul was a master motivator of men. He had to know that these types of men would speak into Timothy's mind in a strong way, and that's exactly what this old warrior's final charge meant to accomplish.

The soldier on active duty never takes a vacation from his responsibilities. He possesses a singular focus: to please his commander. For the soldier, to forget the one who assigned his responsibilities is to forget his identity. He is not free to blend the two identities because, when he enlisted, he gave up his rights. Now he reports within a command structure. He endangers himself and endures hardship, discomfort, deprivation, and untold suffering to earn the title "good soldier."

In his book *Battle Cry*, author Leon Uris takes us on journey of a group of young Marine volunteers from the heartland of America, through boot camp, and eventually to the jungles of the South Pacific. After their first tour in combat they return different men, hardened men, fearless men, having survived malaria, gangrene, and, above all, loss of comrades.

The soldier on active duty never takes a vacation from his responsibilities. He possesses a singular focus: to please his commander.

When a fresh, new replacement arrives, complaining about being drafted, the fraternity of soldiers files out of the room. "Something stinks in here," one of them says on his way out.

The salty sergeant responds to the naive newcomer. "I'll give you some advice. These guys have earned their battle spurs, and you have got a lot of proving to do. They're a good bunch of fellows, and they're big leaguers, and you are just a busher." His point? These guys have endured the hardship of their commitment. They are good soldiers.

The athlete, Paul says, cannot bend the rules to his liking and still expect to win. He can't take shortcuts to get a head start on the competition or adjust things according to his comfort level. He has to compete fairly, respect the boundaries, and run hard just like everybody else for a shot at the prize. The point is, the contest is bigger than any individual athlete. An athlete's primary quality is his respect for the rules. And when he wins legitimately, he has integrity. So he trains right, competes right, and when it's showtime, he focuses on the victor's crown. He dreams of being on that podium, receiving the prize for his hard work and dedication.

Now, a farmer, Paul says, has to be superdiligent in his season of work. He keeps showing up morning after morning, laying those hands to the plow. He doesn't sleep in, and he works late when it's time to sow and cultivate. He will rest *later.* He endures the early wake-up calls, the aching hands, the smells of fertilizer, and the sore legs from walking up and down his fields. He is diligent and determined during the critical time that makes the difference between a good harvest and a bad one. The promise of the harvest spurs him on, because he knows that if he sows sparingly, he will reap sparingly. But that, Paul says, does not happen to the hard-working farmer. He is rewarded with an abundance of crops, which will bless him and many others.

None of this is lost on Timothy. He knows soldiers, athletes, and farmers accept their identities, their responsibilities, and the priorities that accompany them. All three are focused on results, and they have all learned in their unique callings how to endure and choose to resist the temptation to quit. Sure, the soldier could go AWOL. The athlete could use enhancers. The farmer could sleep in. But they've trained themselves over time to perform. They stay focused and keep at it single-mindedly. And they are successful because each has found his motivation: pleasing the commander, winning the prize, and reaping the harvest.

All these profiles fit Jesus's commitment call perfectly. All three deny themselves comfort for their journeys. All three accept responsibility. They pick up their crosses, move forward, and take action to stay loyal, compete, and work hard. All are noble in their own ways, Paul says, but Timothy has to think hard on the implications for his life. If he does, God will spell it out for him.

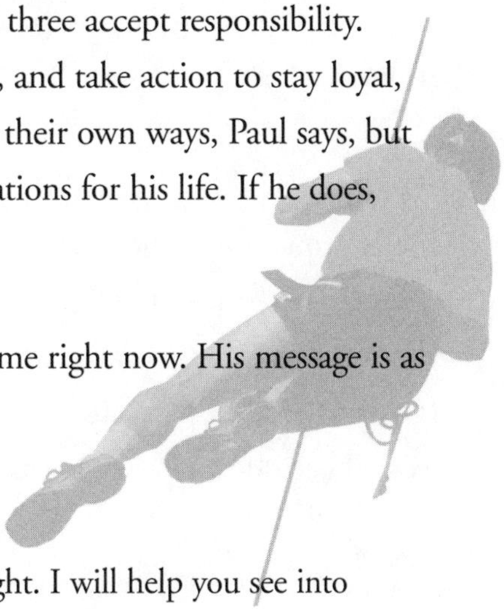

God is saying the same thing to you and me right now. His message is as fresh today to us as it was to Timothy:

> My Son,
>
> Reflect on this. I will give you insight. I will help you see into your own life. I will reveal the implications for you personally and your responsibilities as God's man.
>
> The Lord

Strength and Impact

Paul had two goals for Timothy, and they are the same ones I have for you: that you would be strong and that you would risk making an impact. One is for your spiritual character. The other is for your actions for Christ. One is being; the other is doing. When both come together, you have a powerful witness for Him.

To stay focused as God's men, we must tap the strength of God's grace. Picking his strategy carefully, Paul gave Timothy the secret to a long-lasting witness for Jesus Christ: grace. What saved us is also what sustains us as God's men. If we focus on the love and forgiveness we were given, we become unstoppable for God. No doubt, no fear, no regret. No opinion or prideful thinking can overpower our witness. Its influence over us is too strong.

To stay focused as God's men, we must tap the strength of God's grace.

Paul knew Timothy needed regular reminders of God's grace if he was to finish strong. Over and over Paul motivated followers to use God's love and grace as fuel for the fight. "No," he says to the Roman believers, "in all these things we are more than conquerors through him who loved us" (Romans 8:37). Paul reasons, if we believers can just get this one thing, we will become a force no enemy can overcome.

The power is in the grace. But the impact zone of this internal power is designed to explode outward in ministry. Paul directly connects the ten-megaton grace warhead in the heart of God's man to that natural desire in us to see others experience, understand, and live in that same grace. More specifically, this means all of us are compelled to "pay it forward" by sharing our faith and making disciples. And in doing so, God's man becomes radioactive! For Timothy, this instruction was a natural extension of the masterful model Paul had given him as a recipient and agent of grace.

Like Timothy, God's men need this tactical reminder to stay focused and persevere. Some days will be harder than others, but God is pleased with

His soldier, He rewards His champion, and He brings abundant harvest to His hard-working servant. Timothy had the highest vision and noblest calling, but even this God's man needed to be reminded by another brother that the rewards are worth it.

Brother, nothing is more worth your sacrifice than the Greatest Commandment and the Great Commission. You have His grace. You can let it out. So pay it forward.

chapter 13

spiritual Ebola

I would get a small group of eight or ten or twelve men around me that would meet for a few hours a week and pay the price! I would share with them everything I have, over a period of years. Then I would have twelve ministers who in turn could take eight or ten or twelve more and teach them.

—Billy Graham

Ebola hemorrhagic fever first appeared in the African Congo in 1976. It is caused by infection with Ebola virus, named after the river in Africa where it was first recognized. It is the most feared virus on the planet because, once it infects a person, its ability to spread and cause death is astounding. Some of the better-known and studied outbreaks attest to the power of this tiny viper of death:

- 318 cases in Yambuku, Zaire, in 1976
- 284 cases in Nzara and Maridi, Sudan, in 1976
- 315 cases in Kikwit, Zaire, in 1995

- 425 cases in Gulu, Masindi, and Mbarara, Uganda, in 2000–2001
- 122 cases in Gabon and the Republic of the Congo in 2001–2002

The common denominators of these outbreaks are:

- They are rare. Outbreaks occur sporadically.
- The infection is always acute—there is no "carrier" state.
- The virus is transmitted by close personal contact.
- Outbreaks also occur in contained settings, such as hospitals, where no protective measures are taken. This is called amplification.
- There is an incubation period in a human body of two to twenty-one days.
- Onset of symptoms is abrupt, multiple, and violent.
- The average death rate is over 80 percent.[1]

This last statistic is the one that gives epidemiologists and virologists the heebie-jeebies. They simply do not have a cure—Ebola is an unstoppable systemic force once inside the human body. They can only offer "supportive" care. The best strategy they have for dealing with an outbreak is to isolate it as much as possible—isolate villages, quarantine the infected, and limit contact between the infected and the healthy.

Close Contact

Outbreaks of viral infections like Ebola need to be contained, but good infections, spiritual ones, do not. In fact, Jesus's own life reflected intentional infection with His men—it was needed and necessary if God's plan for the world was to be successful. His life came into close personal contact with ordinary men. Out of the thousands, He intentionally selected and associated with twelve disciples and infected eleven. For three years He downloaded. He gave them everything He had, every chance He had. He deposited:

- Himself—all that He was and was not
- His connection to and experiences with the Father
- His insight into God's Word and life
- His grace and acceptance
- His goals and vision
- His inspiration and encouragement
- His personal call to godliness
- His humanity and vulnerability as a man
- His teaching gifts
- His leadership skills
- His "out of the box" approaches to situations
- His compassion for the lost
- His passion for God's purposes
- His spiritual spine in the face of intimidation
- His willingness to go against the culture in order to be God's man
- His sense of people, their needs, and how to meet them
- His ministry of teaching, preaching, healing, and sharing God's love
- His authority and commission
- His willingness to sacrifice

"Everyone, after he has been fully trained, will be like his teacher" (Luke 6:40, NASB), Jesus told his trainees. His end game was infection. His actions were deliberate, and He wanted His men to possess His mission, share His feelings on things, and imitate His behavior. His way was God's way, and that was what made Him confident and contagious. His men were in contact, exposed, caught Him, got infected, and, ultimately, would spread this way of living like wildfire to everyone in their paths.

Jesus knew that the measure of His mission would be His ability to reproduce Himself. Otherwise the mission would not get done. Jesus did a lot of public healings, preached to the masses, and fed thousands, but His goal was to train a few guys who would go out and multiply the message and ministry way beyond His time on earth. He knew only a few needed to be truly infected. Are you? Then you need to think like Jesus did and risk infecting others on purpose. You also need to be wise about it. Here's how to think about it.

Jesus's own life reflected intentional infection with His men—it was needed and necessary if God's plan for the world was to be successful.

Imagine you are a great evangelist (like Billy Graham great) and share your faith with one person every day of every year for sixteen straight years. Assuming all those people accept the message and commit their lives to Christ, you will have led 5,840 into a personal relationship with Christ. It's simple addition. Not bad. You might say, "No, unbelievable!" Now imagine that you train or disciple two people in year one, and they train two people each in year two and so on. In year sixteen, because your training curve is multiplying geometrically rather than merely adding arithmetically, you will have infected 65,536 people. That's unbelievable, but that's the Jesus way. Jesus did His math and knew that multiplication would get the job done faster and better than addition.

Fact time: God's man is made to reproduce.

Reclaiming the Core Urge

Danny Wallen is the director of ministry at Every Man Ministries. We call him Yoda around here because every time he opens his mouth, you feel stupid. I usually have a pencil and pad handy when he goes off in a stream of consciousness because the dude knows how to raise up and train men.

One day, standing in my doorway, he dropped his pearls on me about how men are wired by God with an urge to reproduce. He said,

> The most natural and positive thing for a man is to reproduce. God made us that way. Think about it. Why do you think we are consciously and subconsciously driven by our sexual impulses? We seek to connect, reproduce, procreate, and multiply! I know it sounds funny, but it is true. It is the most natural impulse we have, which gets the lion's share of our energy over a lifetime. This instinct is systemic, subconscious, and powerful. The problem is that men don't translate their natural drive to reproduce into a spiritual reproduction, because sin and fear have conflicted and polluted our desires. Sexual success, material success, and professional success have replaced relational success and spiritual multiplication. For most men, momentary attachments define us instead of our generational impact.

Ouch, Danny. I'm not sure whether to be glad I wrote this down or not. Sex and discipleship? Are you hiding a crack pipe?

Then I think back to my college experience, and I have two examples of men who trained other men as effortlessly and strongly as guys in my fraternity ogled and engaged the babes of Westwood. Matt Booker and J. P. Jones invested themselves in training me on the UCLA campus in the early eighties. Of course it didn't feel like training at all, but make no mistake, training was happening.

It all started in my dorm room in Hedrick Hall with a phone call from Matt. It was the fall of 1982, and he asked to have coffee with me. I ended up meeting with Matt individually once a week and with a small group of fraternity guys who were believers to go through the essentials of the Christian life. Matt was a UCLA graduate, was in a fraternity, and could relate to my wild past. Every Saturday I would hear his white Fiat sputtering outside the dorm at 7:00 a.m. to take me and a few other guys to Papa Pete's breakfast house. J.P. was there too. Between the $1.85 ham and eggs scramble with a side of pancakes, the lousy coffee, and witnessing to the waitresses, I was learning how to be a disciple. I had a special connection to Matt but also knew that I was part of a fellowship of men.

The most natural and positive thing for a man is to reproduce. God made us that way.

It may have been the eighties, but the texture of these relationships was very first century. Jesus was inside these two godly men bringing me to maturity and training me to eventually train others. It was not a "program"; it was a way of life that was very attractive. These guys made investing your life in another man for the purposes of spiritual growth as natural as breathing. Every one of us thought: *This is what we are supposed to be doing.* That year I saw what a disciple looked like, and I liked what I saw. Matt showed me how to study God's Word, how to share my faith, how to be filled and directed by the Holy Spirit, and how to lead others in a small group. Most of this I learned by tagging along, and Jesus was pleased with Matt.

My sophomore year I was handed off to J.P., which was different. While Matt had a heart for mentoring and evangelism, J.P. was like a human Bible dictionary trapped in a linebacker's body. I loved it when I would meet with him and just pepper him with my stupid questions about all aspects of life, which, at that time, consisted mainly of God and girls. School was a distant third. For J.P., however, school was at the forefront—seminary, that is. Fortunately, we in his Bible study were his lab to test out all that good theology. We sucked him dry! Forget about the fact that he wore a pink Polo shirt, jeans, and bathed in Ralph Lauren cologne or that he was dirt poor. We loved him because he would take us to the beach or to a mountain retreat and teach us all he knew about God, life, and his favorite movie lines.

Jesus was inside these two godly men bringing me to maturity and training me to eventually train others. It was not a "program"; it was a way of life that was very attractive.

Eventually, J.P. challenged all the guys in the group to teach the Bible at our weekly campus meetings. The first message I ever preached, with J.P.'s assistance, was to five hundred students, where, at the end of the message, I gave them an invitation to personally commit their lives to Christ. I was terrified of speaking in front of that many people, but J.P. sat down with me and helped me prepare my message. Twenty-five students gave their lives to Christ that fall night at UCLA. In large measure, they have J.P. to thank for being obedient to God's call and investing himself in the life of a young Christian man. He had me reproducing, and I knew then that I would be doing this the rest of my life in some form. He showed me how to make a disciple and that I needed to do the same.

Just this last year I took a group of men who were new believers through the same material J.P. took me through over twenty years ago. Nothing fancy, just doing life together, opening God's Word, and trying to model what it means to be God's man. These men are Matt Booker's and J. P. Jones's spiritual progeny—Matt and J.P. are grandparents in the faith of these I had the privilege to lead to the Lord and mentor. They, too, are now reproducing, so I guess that makes Matt and J.P. great-grandparents of the newly born fruit.

God's man needs to be trained to worship, connect, grow, serve, and share his faith in a deliberately relational way by another man. This is what you were made to do.

You might be reading this and saying, "Good for you, but I don't have anybody like that in my life. I have never been discipled or trained by another man." If this is you, it's time to risk seeking out and securing that relationship or that pathway with another man. You cannot become God's man in a vacuum. The disciples needed Jesus. Timothy, Epaphras, Titus, and Mark needed Paul. I needed J.P. and Matt. Tony, Kevin, Tim, and Ali needed me. God's man needs to be trained to worship, connect, grow, serve, and share his faith in a deliberately relational way by another man. This is what you were made to do.

So, God's man, who is the Matt or J.P. in your life? Who could it *possibly* be? Can you name a candidate? Are you willing to risk being trained to reproduce? Are you contagious?

Make Deposits

Got a bank account? Make deposits? Make withdrawals? Spend money? If so, you'll have no problem connecting with the biblical concept of discipleship and reproduction.

The majority of us entrust the safekeeping of our money to financial institutions. Our funds are put there for safekeeping so that we don't misplace them or get robbed of our cash. Every time we receive a paycheck, most of us fill out a deposit slip, bring it to the teller, and make sure it's credited to our account. Or we wire the money electronically from our employer to our bank in the form of an automatic deposit. However your money gets there, you trust it to be there for you to use when you need cash, write a check, or use your debit card. If you are like me, the money goes into your checking account through a deposit, you write checks or use your debit card, and then money is deposited into someone else's bank account. All of us are players.

When it came to being a disciple, the apostle Paul looked at the men he touched much like banks that have been entrusted with the valuable commodities of his spiritual investments. While held prisoner in Rome by the emperor Nero, Paul made sure one of his best trainees remembered how precious the investment of his life was to him. The trainee, Timothy, was a spiritual repository of Paul's best thinking, modeling, ministry. And message. These needed to be both guarded and preserved by Timothy, as well as multiplied like an investment into the lives of others.

First, he had to value what Paul taught him. "What you heard from me, keep as the pattern of sound teaching, with faith and love in Christ Jesus. Guard the good deposit that was entrusted to you—guard it with the help of the Holy Spirit who lives in us" (2 Timothy 1:13–14). There was a pattern of thinking and teaching that Paul passed down to his disciple Timothy while they were together over the years that Timothy needed to retain, protect, and preserve in the life he lived among others he would influence for Christ. As God's man, Timothy needed to "keep the pattern" he had learned from another God's man in terms of the message he was to share with others. Timothy needed to guard the deposit Paul made in his life rather than squander or waste it.

Timothy needed to guard the deposit Paul made in his life rather than squander or waste it.

After making a commitment to value and safeguard the message and truth deposited into his life, Timothy needed to take one more step: give it away to other men and multiply his impact generationally for Christ. Just a few sentences later in this same letter, he is told not just to guard the deposit but to *make deposits* in the lives of other men.

> So, my son, throw yourself into this work for Christ. Pass on what you heard from me—the whole congregation saying Amen!—to reliable leaders who are competent to teach others. When the going gets rough, take it on the chin with the rest of us, the way Jesus did. A soldier on duty doesn't get caught up in making deals at the mar-

> ketplace. He concentrates on carrying out orders. An athlete who refuses to play by the rules will never get anywhere. It's the diligent farmer who gets the produce. Think it over. God will make it all plain. (2 Timothy 2:1–7, MSG)

It was gonna take some thinking, but the call was crystal clear: "Reproduce yourself, Timothy." I am glad Paul gave his man a little space to breathe and think, because few men have the commitment and guts to give their lives away by investing them (without guarantees) into the lives of other men. Timothy had seen Paul disappointed on more than one occasion by men who bailed on their training to chase other passions. On the other hand, he had seen firsthand how well equipped he was due to the training and experiences he'd received while traveling with Paul. He was the head pastor of a huge church in his twenties! The people Timothy would train would in turn multiply, reproduce, and expand his impact in ways that he would never see this side of eternity. But like the farmer who diligently works, the harvest would be his.

Paul defined discipleship in the simplest and most functional sense: it's taking another man on a spiritual journey with you.

As Timothy was thinking it over, I bet he reflected on when he first met Paul. As any good leader would, the great apostle was looking for his replacement, and he had heard things about the kid from Lystra, so he decided to check him out. It must have seemed liked yesterday. Rewind to how they connected:

> He came to Derbe and then to Lystra, where a disciple named Timothy lived, whose mother was a Jewess and a believer, but whose father was a Greek. The brothers at Lystra and Iconium spoke well

> of him. Paul wanted to take him along on the journey, so he circumcised him because of the Jews who lived in that area, for they all knew that his father was Greek. As they traveled from town to town, they delivered the decisions reached by the apostles and elders in Jerusalem for the people to obey. So the churches were strengthened in the faith and grew daily in numbers. (Acts 16:1–5)

Paul defined discipleship in the simplest and most functional sense: it's taking another man on a spiritual journey with you. He grabbed Timothy, took him for outpatient surgery, and hit the road! Those early days must have been flooding Timothy's mind as he read Paul's letter penned from a dungeon in Rome. They traveled together, taught together, ate many a meal together, laughed I'm sure, saw a huge number of people come to know Jesus personally. Paul selected Timothy, but at this moment Timothy must have thought about how God had put the whole relationship together for this very moment in his life.

Raising up and training a leader to do God's work is nuclear—it has a blast zone that extends to people you will never know you impacted.

Risking reproducing yourself spiritually requires guts and perseverance, but it is also the greatest adventure God's man will ever take. Raising up and training a leader to do God's work is nuclear—it has a blast zone that extends to people you will never know you impacted. All because you invested yourself and made deposits into the life of one other person and intentionally brought him to maturity in order to release him to ministry. People touching people…who touch people…for Jesus in a chain of relationships that spans *centuries.*

As a men's pastor, I am fascinated with the whole idea of one man infecting another and causing an outbreak. This is my goal for the men in my church—that they be contagious reproducers. The reason why is that Jesus was all about infecting a few men during His brief time on earth who would then in turn infect a world. Paul had the same mentality. Matt and J.P. too. How about you? When God's man decides to give away what he knows to other men, he sets in motion a chain reaction.

Who's going to be in your chain?

chapter 14

the first two seconds

The voice of God is a friendly voice. No one need fear to listen to it unless he has already made up his mind to resist it.

—A. W. Tozer

Good decisions do not require great deliberation.

In his book *Blink,* author Malcolm Gladwell bravely points out that great decisions come about by an ability we all have to quickly filter out the most meaningful factors from the irrelevant. He calls it "rapid cognition" and "thin-slicing." We might call it a gut feeling or a guiding instinct. If you read his stuff, you are going to feel validated as a man, even euphoric, because he validates the masculine way of decision making—my style of decision making—quick!

However, he doesn't stop there. He goes on to explain how our experiences and our environments inform this ability for better or for worse. There is a huge gap, for example, between blind impulses and trained intuition. This means we can use this ability responsibly or irresponsibly.

One style works against us, and the other rescues us. Whether you are confronting a complex situation or have to make a decision under stress, the message is this: you don't have to see *all* the variables to make great spontaneous decisions, you just have to see the most important ones. With the right filters, Gladwell's research shows, you can zero in on what really matters, develop a sense of smell, and move on instinct with clarity and confidence.

What fascinated me was that the research shows how we can train ourselves into good "gut instincts" to achieve specific and more noble goals.

> Our first impressions are generated by our experiences and our environment, which means that we can change our first impressions—we can alter the way we thin-slice—by changing the experiences that comprise those impressions. If you are a white person who would like to treat black people as equals in every way—who would like to have a set of associations with blacks that are as positive as those that you have with whites—it requires more than a simple commitment to equality. It requires that you change your life so that you are exposed to minorities on a regular basis and become comfortable with them and familiar with the best of their culture, so that when you want to meet, hire, date, or talk with a member of a minority, you aren't betrayed by your hesitation and discomfort. Taking rapid cognition seriously—acknowledging the incredible power, for good or ill, that first impressions play in our lives—requires that we take active steps to manage and control those impressions.[1]

Gladwell's point: changed experiences and changed exposures lead to changed impressions and better reactions under pressure when making decisions. The amazing ability of the brain to quickly analyze and deliver the necessary output to make good choices assumes that there are some moral disciplines (or in our case, spiritual disciplines) and actions previously taken which are feeding our intuition in the moment. These "thin slices" help us take charge in the first two seconds of any given situation. The big question for all of us is: What is the substance of our experiences and environments that guides us in these critical moments? What's filtering our reactions and responses? Can we trust it to help us as God's men?

Exposed in the Moment

Jesus was a man who demonstrated that He could think on His feet. The Gospels reveal a man who could sift through a situation, person, or mob, throw out all that was irrelevant, and target the core issue or necessary action. His answers to things were not exhaustive, and His methods were unorthodox at times, but they were always consistent with His goals and mission as the Son of God. Above all, He never panicked in the face of pressure or wavered in the moment. He was grace and truth. He was silk and, when needed, steel. Marvel at the following situations, statements, and actions of Jesus. Talk about rapid cognition!

The Gospels reveal a man who could sift through a situation, person, or mob, throw out all that was irrelevant, and target the core issue or necessary action.

Jesus Christ owned the first two seconds of any situation, demonstrating how God's man can discern clearly without thinking when put on the spot:

- By those seeking to trap Him: "One of them, an expert in the law, tested him with this question: 'Teacher, which is the greatest commandment in the Law?' Jesus replied, ' "Love the Lord your God with all your heart and with all your soul and with all your mind." This is the first and greatest commandment. And the second is like it: "Love your neighbor as yourself." All the Law and the Prophets hang on these two commandments' " (Matthew 22:35–40).
- By the devil's proposition: "The devil said to him, 'If you are the Son of God, tell this stone to become bread.' Jesus answered, 'It is written: "Man does not live on bread alone" ' " (Luke 4:3–4).
- By a mob presenting a woman caught in the act of adultery: " 'Teacher, this woman was caught in the act of adultery. In the Law Moses commanded us to stone such women. Now what do you say?' They were using this question as a trap, in order to have a basis for accusing him. But Jesus bent down and started to write on the ground with his finger. When they kept on questioning him, he straightened up and said to them, 'If any one of you is without sin, let him be the first to throw a stone at her' " (John 8:4–7).
- In the middle of a family conflict: "Martha was distracted by all the preparations that had to be made. She came to him and asked, 'Lord, don't you care that my sister has left me to do the work by myself? Tell her to help me!' 'Martha, Martha,' the Lord answered, 'you are worried and upset about many things, but only one thing is needed. Mary has chosen what is better, and it will not be taken away from her' " (Luke 10:40–42).

Both Jesus's private life and public life were loaded with moments that required special intuition and efficient, God-honoring responses. Sound familiar?

- confrontations with the competition
- personal temptations when emotionally and physically weak
- interruptions in your workflow
- comparison to others
- badgering and harassment
- people placed on your porch with big life issues and problems
- dysfunctional family blowups
- needing to speak the truth when it's going to sting the other person

No long, involved deliberations. No codependency. No overprocessing. No sophisticated mental engineering in shaping His responses. No confusion. No anger. No sweat—not a drop.

What we clearly see is a man whose experiences, exposures, and environments had created an intuition He could trust and that performed. His relationship with His Father, His understanding of His purposes, His encounters with real needs of people, His investments of time and energy in the disciples, His service to others, and His strong sense of identity made Him free and successful in spontaneous situations. When called upon to improvise, Jesus thrived because He had a strong adherence to a simple framework: love God and love people. He was free under pressure because He was committed to never denying loyalty and love for His Father and serving people. "My food...is to do the will of him who sent me" (John 4:34) and the "Son of Man did not come to be served, but to serve" (Mark

When called upon to improvise, Jesus thrived because He had a strong adherence to a simple framework: love God and love people.

10:45) are the kinds of statements coming from the mouth of the God-Man that reflect the general character of His experiences and environments that shaped His intuition at any given moment.

Free in the Fight

General George S. Patton Jr. once said, “I love the smell of a battlefield.” The reason he could say this was because he had the ability to both see and make sense of it intuitively. A lifetime devoted to the study of warfare and multiple field combat experiences gave him this nose. More important, he was guided by a set of principles when prosecuting a war that he believed in with every atom of his being.

The two things you see repeatedly expressed in his philosophy of warfare are the emphasis on planning and, when the time came for battle, “attack rapidly, ruthlessly, viciously, without rest, however tired and hungry you may be, the enemy will be more tired and more hungry. Keep punching.” This was Patton’s simple and effective constitution concerning warfare, the indestructible foundation, his filter for decision making. Formidable enemies, disagreeable bureaucrats, lopsided numbers, unforgiving terrain, and complicated schemes were all beside the point if he felt he had the right plan and his men could violently execute it. His certainty wasn’t so much ego as it was strength of his belief in his philosophy of war. He knew this was the way to do bat-

> ***He knew this was the way to do battle, and believing as he did, he eliminated distractions, detractors, and doubt from his line of vision. He was free in the fight.***

tle, and believing as he did, he eliminated distractions, detractors, and doubt from his line of vision. He was free in the fight.

Most men lack such freedom in the fight to do battle as God's man. This is in large part because they haven't understood how to create it. That is why I encourage men around the world to risk becoming purpose-driven men who arrange their lives around:

- knowing and loving God
- connecting to other God's men
- becoming like Christ
- having a ministry to believers
- reaching out to those without Christ

This is what forms your identity and provides experiences that train your intuition. Men who are committed to arranging their lives around these purposes are free in the fight, because God's way eliminates confusion and provides clear decisions and godly instincts for effectiveness.

Whether you're sizing up a decision, a relationship, or a particular circumstance, God's man, devoted fully to God's purposes, will not need a long list of options. Instead, he will target what really matters based on his exposure and experiences with God's purposes. His filters have changed. For God's man this means deciding things differently and always choosing:

- loyalty to God over man
- connection over isolation
- character of Christ over comfort

- serving God's people over self
- speaking up about Christ's influence in his life over remaining silent
- choosing the principles in the Word over those of the world
- hearing the Spirit's voice over the flesh's whispers

A man who risks committing himself fully to these purposes, consciously builds his life around them, and keeps punching will not be mastered by any earthly moment. He might get stunned or knocked down, but he will come out punching and land more blows. Why? Because he sees the most important variables in a given situation: what shows love for God and what demonstrates love for people. Extra information is unnecessary because godly instincts are in charge. Instead of making messes, he is discerning without thinking and making things better around him.

More Intuition, Less Impulse

Holy hunches. Sensing the Spirit. Trusting insight over eyesight. All this talk sounds ethereal and spooky to a lot of men because it requires faith—and risk. If you are God's man, Gladwell's research confirms what you should already know—God's Spirit is not failing in your life. In fact, He is constantly providing direction and communication. The problem is not with Him; it's with us. God speaks to our minds and provides opportunities for spiritual rapid cognition. The disparity between intuition and impulse lies in our familiarity with His voice. If we're hearing His voice, we cannot give in to our impulses. He might be speaking loudly, but we often press the mute button in the moment out of the habit of serving impulses rather than spiritual intuition. Make no mistake—God has you reading this exactly because He wants you to stop muting the voice of the Holy Spirit in your life and start being a first-time listener. He wants you to exercise your intuition rather than your impulses.

Here's how to say yes to the Holy Spirit:

1. *Desire to please God.* The bottom line of all spiritual progress begins here. "No more stumbling around. Get on with it! The good, the right, the true—these are the actions appropriate for daylight hours. Figure out what will please Christ, and then do it" (Ephesians 5:8–10, MSG).
2. *Recognize and surrender to His role in your life on an increasing basis.* "So, as the Holy Spirit says: 'Today, if you hear his voice, do not harden your hearts,' " wrote the author of Hebrews to early Christians who are about to make a big mistake in their walk with the Lord (3:7–8). There's nothing confusing here: that voice telling you to do it God's way instead of your way is the Holy Spirit! Are you getting a repeated thought consistent with God's purposes, feeling led to do something for your faith, or being prompted by godly men in your life to take a certain action? Take it! The main issue is control, and we need to learn how to surrender early and often to His control and influence, not live the impulse-driven life.
3. *Go under His influence now.* Prayer is how God's man initiates, activates, and applies the Holy Spirit's abilities in his life. Sincerely read this prayer expressing your desire to go under the control of the Spirit, and pray it earnestly and often: *Holy Spirit, I know I need You. I know that I am tempted to be in control of my life, and when I am, I miss out on Your wonderful plan. I am sorry for taking over when I shouldn't or muting Your voice so that I*

Make no mistake—God has you reading this exactly because He wants you to stop muting the voice of the Holy Spirit in your life and start being a first-time listener.

can sin. I surrender. Take control of my life right now and fill me. Speak to me loudly, lead me, guide me, open my eyes to God's plan, and help me choose it quickly. Thank You for taking control. In Jesus's name I ask. Amen.

4. *Recognize that discomfort is the Holy Spirit signaling you to make a choice for God.* The role of the Holy Spirit in the life of God's man is to make him uneasy and uncomfortable when there is a choice on the line for self versus God. When anything can take your relationships with God and people into a pit, the Holy Spirit will automatically flood your mind with warnings, passages of Scripture, people, or circumstances designed to give you a spiritual fever. You will feel uncomfortable about making a decision. He doesn't need to raise His voice when you are deciding to eat a bite of food or put on clothes. However, He will prompt you, convict you, and remind you if you are contemplating a porn site or skipping your time in His Word. If you learn to recognize this spiritual discomfort, you will be cooperating with the Holy Spirit more and experience more freedom.

If you learn to recognize this spiritual discomfort, you will be cooperating with the Holy Spirit more and experience more freedom.

5. *Take right actions in spite of feelings.* The key to winning moments is the first few seconds. Prompt (versus delayed) obedience is critical. When we obey without listening to conflicting feelings, we are trusting God. When I'm camping with my kids and I see something dangerous they don't, I call their name, call them over, and explain after. I expect them to listen to my voice over their feelings about continuing their own way. Because there is a trust there, they do an about-face when I call. That's why the Bible tells God's man to pay

close attention, trust, and keep the communication channels wide open: "Since we live by the Spirit, let us keep in step with the Spirit" (Galatians 5:25). So are you? Keeping in step with the Spirit today? Watching for His leading and following His direction without questioning?

Here's how to know you are keeping in step with the Holy Spirit:

- You're saying no to impulses and feelings and yes to your intuition.
- You're taking God at His Word without delay.
- You're experiencing freedom from habits that frees your relationships.
- You're recognizing rather than rejecting the conviction of the Spirit.
- You're connecting more with God's people.
- You're sharing God's work in your life with others more.
- You're honest with God, honest with yourself, and honest with others.
- You're caring less what others think and more what God thinks.
- Your focus has moved from your needs to others'.
- Others are noticing you're different.

Gladwell is right. Great decisions do not require great deliberation. For God's man, great decisions require simple cooperation in the first few seconds. That voice will always say, "Honor God and love people." So the next time you encounter a complex situation, listen to your godly instinct and obey it—quickly.

chapter 15

suit up and show up

When everything else is on the line, you better be there too.

—DEACON JONES

My mom passed away this year.

It was only thirty days from diagnosis to burial. I had been waiting for that call from the Sacramento area code. I knew it would be my sister Debbie. I knew it would be at an odd time. I knew what she was going to say. I knew we would run the same emotional gamut as we had with my dad just a few years earlier. I knew that we would all take it very, very hard. What I did not know was how God would call my brother and me to lead the family through an end of an era.

While there are many lessons mortality taught me, one thing I experienced through the four-week process—from the grave news to the gravesite—was the power of spiritual leadership.

You might think, *Whoa! Isn't that missing the point? Isn't death supposed to be about sadness, grief, heaven, loss, family, tears, good-byes, family togetherness, and the like?* Absolutely. I entered all those processes the moment I got the call from Debbie about mom's going in for a scan because, as she put it, "Something wasn't right on the inside." In fact, as I was going through the odyssey of my mother's final chapter of life, I wasn't thinking of spiritual leadership or a chapter in a book. I was simply doing my best to get a grip on the needs of the moment and how I was supposed to feel, respond, or react.

Only *after* going through the whole range of situations, interactions, crises, emotions, and issues was I able to look back and see something profound and powerful about the journey. It started with a question from my ol' pal Jeff (Jefferooni to me). The day I got back from Sacramento, he asked, "So, Kenny, what was something that really sticks out in your mind about the process?"

My response surprised even me as these words poured through weakened levees of my brain and over my lips: "The power of spiritual leadership."

Naturally, Jeff said, "Really? Why?" with a puzzled expression. I met that look with one of my own that moment—pure confidence and clarity.

For Such a Time as This

Crises demand good leadership or else people suffer. For my family this was a crisis not just of health but of many other things. This wasn't like losing a distant aunt or uncle, this was my mom—an end of an era for our clan. A few things the family was experiencing were:

- *A crisis of relationships.* Who would step in to make sure that mom's dying wish of family unity was fulfilled? Family relationships were fragmented.
- *A crisis of community.* Who would be there to represent the family and respond to the outpouring of sympathy with a message of gratitude and a story of hope that honored my mom and Jesus Christ? We needed strong family ambassadors.
- *A crisis of energy.* Who would relieve my sisters from caring 24/7 for mom when she came home from the hospital and into hospice care? We needed some heavy lifters.
- *A crisis of eternal implications.* Who would make sure mom was going to heaven? We needed to see her confess her faith in Christ.
- *A crisis of loss.* Who would be there to make sure the pain of the loss and God's purposes in that loss would be discovered? We needed to experience God's plan through this time.

From the first call alerting the family to mom's condition, my brother, Chris, and I were on the phone. While the logistics stuff (medicine, care, funeral arrangements, the family trust, and so on) was squarely in my sisters' laps (they lived near Mom), my brother and I felt the burden to, as Chris puts it, "suit up and show up" for Jesus in this situation. That meant:

- canceling our schedules indefinitely
- taking over shifts from my sisters
- cooking (mostly Chris)
- changing my mom's diapers (it took the two of us)
- praying on every occasion
- ministering to my mom's family

- leaving our families, businesses, and deadlines unattended to honor mom
- affirming and encouraging family members
- recognizing and ministering to the tender hearts in the family
- bringing the family to God's promises and perspectives
- grieving hard
- helping mom let go to embrace her new beginning
- sharing the gospel at her memorial

Crises call for redeemers—men who will step in and convert otherwise hopeless situations into ones of value, opportunity, and power. Crises require forces for good—men made of the good stuff who will give away what's inside for God and for people. Crises demand men of truth—men who are authentic, not synthetic and shallow. Crises need real beliefs and convictions that transcend the loss to provide hope—men with a message that offers perspective in the midst of the pain. Crises worsen without leadership—men plunge into emotional, relational, and spiritual darkness as evil forces prevail in the absence of the light and life a good leader provides by his mere presence.

Crises demand good leadership or else people suffer. Crises call for redeemers.

To be clear, Chris and I are your last candidates for knighthood. We have pasts. We have regrets. We've "stepped in it" hundreds of times—just ask our wives. But both of us have committed to becoming God's man in our personal lives. Which means we:

- pursue God's purposes, not our own
- are led by the promises and truth in His Word

- have experienced the deepest forgiveness available
- are fearless about the future
- are dedicated to serve and love others
- speak of heaven with confidence
- are ambassadors of the gospel and its power to save
- speak truth in love
- work for peace in relationships
- hate sin and the separation it creates
- step out in faith when others question
- leave room for the Holy Spirit to do His thing before we do ours

For Chris and me, blood brothers became brothers *of the blood.* We had the code of Christ in common, and we flew the flag of the King. For this hour, in this family and this situation, we knew this moment was made for us to lead. That's what God trained us for, and we were listening to orders, dutifully executing them for our family at every turn.

We risked aggressive leadership as God's men.

The result? Miracle after miracle after miracle in a very dark hour. Like shiny diamonds on black velvet, the glory of God came in to redeem death, destruction, discord, and despair. These were replaced with family renewal, recommitments, reconciliation, and relational unity. Conversations and loving confrontations. Prayers, tears, and hugs. Words of counsel, party preparations, grocery trips, supernatural patience, and just being near and listening. These were the invitations God supplied. All these in honor of my

For this hour, in this family and this situation, we knew this moment was made for us to lead.

mother in her journey to eternity, allowing her to pass freely without a concern about her future or her children's, grandchildren's, and great-grandchildren's futures.

The funny thing is that none of this was a huge exertion. I felt as though I was born to step up to this. Under the heavy load of circumstances, I felt free to speak and act according to my training as God's man. And Chris felt the same. We kept encouraging each other, "Just be God's man, buddy." Each day, we would assess our responses and affirm each other, praying for more of God's power. We were exhausted and emotionally drained but never insecure or without reserves to meet the challenges. Now Chris and I stand back and marvel about that time—we tell stories about it like two old men reminiscing about a defining battle.

I think what we're proud of is that our family got the chance to see the many days, months, and years of training. Before, it might have been misunderstood or misrepresented, but through that time all doubt was erased about us and who we were. We were able to say, *This is what being God's man is all about.* Consequently, my sisters and other family members were able to relax and grieve. One sister, through tears, told us, "You have no idea how thankful I am for what you have done. We could never have made it though this the way we did without you and Chris."

That felt good. Mission accomplished.

Special Ops

Navy SEAL. Army Ranger. Delta Force. Do you love these guys as much as I do? The mystique. The bravery. The stealthy missions. The skills. The risks!

I confess. I'm a sucker for any good warrior doing a good thing for his country, but these guys are "special," which is why they've been given the unique label of Special Forces by the Defense Department. Their label reflects the nature of their missions, which are uncommon and unusual, mostly because the potential for loss of life is high if the slightest mistakes are made.

If a soldier is caught behind enemy lines, for example, these guys get the call. If a terrorist cell is discovered and poses a lethal threat to the safety and security of our country, these men in black are called in. If reconnaissance is needed on the enemy and detection is not an option, these guys are camouflaged and dropped in from the stratosphere and *left there* for long periods. Special needs require special missions by special men trained and equipped to do what's necessary under pressure to achieve their country's objectives. They have a mission, and behind their mission is a cause—usually freedom for someone or something.

The spirit of these warriors is like the spirit of God's men. In fact, when God finds a man who is passionate for His purposes, trained in the Word, filled with the Spirit, humble in heart, He will send that man into situations unsuited for others. The men, like the missions, are different, even odd, but they are custom-trained for these jobs—jobs only they can do. Wondrously stunned God's men have said to me, "If you'd have asked me ten years ago if I'd be doing this, I would've said you were crazy or something real close."

I know what they mean. I felt the same way speaking at a Promise Keepers convention on masturbation. I started off by saying, "Just because I am speaking on masturbation does not mean I am an expert in the subject!" All kidding aside, my testimony today is pretty peculiar: from being a guy who *was* pretty good at it, through the struggle to overcome lust and shame, to traveling around the world talking to men about masturbation, sexual integrity, marriage, and intimacy, to writing books about it. Had you tried to tell me it would happen, I would have spit my drink all over your shirt! But God *did* make me for this unique mission in the world. I am a part of His special forces.

When God finds a man who is passionate for His purposes, trained in the Word, filled with the Spirit, humble in heart, He will send that man into situations unsuited for others.

Today, I'm called on to do certain missions that only I am trained and equipped for. God tactically places me in certain groups of men, pastors, seats on airplanes, on college campuses, soccer fields, cars, offices, and countless situations to help others see God or experience His plan in their situation—masturbators included! Can you see why I love my life? What an adventure!

Imagine this. God's love expresses itself through us when we do what He asks us to do. Thousands upon thousands of these moments present themselves, multiplying over the span of a lifetime, and we choose to live life either God's way or our own way. But some moments are distinguishable from others, like when you are called on to exert influence, take action, have a conversation, or rescue a person for Jesus Christ. These are the times you know you need to lead spiritually:

- A married co-worker tells you he's about to have an affair.
- The stranger beside you is reading a book and needs to consider the gospel rather than a self-help guru.

- Your wife wants to spend the month's tithe on putting in the new floor.
- Your brother-in-law has an alcohol problem and his family is suffering.
- Your friend is suicidal and he calls to tell *you.*
- A family member's salvation is uncertain.
- Bitterness is destroying a family relationship.
- You have a vision for a project that will honor God.
- You've been approached to support a ministry project and have the resources to respond.
- Your community has a need you know how to meet.
- Your church is participating in a relief effort and they need a leader.
- The guys in your couples group need to connect as men.

The common denominator in all these situations is that *someone* needs to step up! Someone needs to be the unselfish leader. Someone needs to sacrifice. Someone needs to stop caring about being rejected or inconvenienced. Someone needs to meet the need. Someone needs to open his mouth. Someone needs to be bold. Someone needs to stop fearing the consequences and trust in God.

Brother, that someone is *you.*

You've been saved from yourself, connected to God's Holy Spirit, and inserted tactically into life and relationships to accomplish these missions.

You, God's man, are alive at a certain time in history, placed on a certain part of the globe, given your own unique testimony, and endowed with natural and spiritual abilities. This is not by chance. You've been saved from yourself, connected to God's Holy Spirit, and inserted tactically into life and relationships to accomplish these missions. Some may seem innocuous. Others are obviously volatile. But make no mistake, this is the mentality of God's men.

The original God-Man knew why He was here, and we, under His leadership, should think the same when it comes to our mission on earth. On earth, Jesus was focused and mindful that the mission window was closing and He needed to seize the moment. More important, He wanted His men to see the urgent need to fulfill *their* mission even as He was committed to His own.

> His disciples urged him, "Rabbi, eat something."
>
> But he said to them, "I have food to eat that you know nothing about."
>
> Then his disciples said to each other, "Could someone have brought him food?"
>
> "My food," said Jesus, "is to do the will of him who sent me and to finish his work." (John 4:31–34)

"Hey, Sarge, can't we stop for a burger?" The reply must have caught them a bit off guard and left them a little embarrassed. He told them in no uncertain terms that what sustained Him and compelled Him was the mission. He had been sent, and He would finish.

I often wonder how many missions God has sent His men into that were left unfinished because of an inability to see the situation clearly. How many windows of opportunity have been missed? Let's be honest, that should scare the snot out of every God's man called to serve and lead. I never want my men at Saddleback to miss their mission windows or relax when they need to be focused. I tell them they have to look at themselves as God's special forces, divinely inserted, specifically tasked, and spiritually equipped to redeem the lost causes from the talons of the Enemy. They need to walk into, not out of, situations that require any kind of leadership. They need to ignore distorting voices and fears, stay ready for the signal to act, and move in swiftly when called. At any hour of any day, they could be called on to apply their training as God's men for God's purposes.

This is how God's man thinks. He accepts assignments, and he finishes them. Big or small, significant or trivial, they are his responsibility to execute.

Fact time: we are not our own and we *need* to lead.

You might wonder, *What does this mean for me here and now?* It might mean you go to your local bookstore and pick up *Every Man, God's Man.* I wrote that book to give Christ-followers a template for how to live and think consistent with their faith in today's culture. You might need to turn to God in prayer right now and ask His forgiveness for shirking responsibility. You might need to lock arms with a band of brothers and share a vision to meet a need. You might need to apologize to your family for not leading them and make a new commitment to action instead of words. You might need to step right into the middle of a huge mess you have been avoiding because it meant time, emotions, money, or confrontation. In any case, you need to step up, not as a spiritually neutral party but as an ambassador of the King.

The apostle Paul would have made an outstanding Delta Force commando. He thought like one, but more important, he lived like one. He didn't live for man but for the Supreme Commander. "The most important thing is that I complete my mission, the work that the Lord Jesus gave me—to tell people the Good News about God's grace" (Acts 20:24, NCV). This is how God's man thinks. He accepts assignments, and he finishes them. Big or small, significant or trivial, they are his responsibility to execute.

To think like this requires a different perspective toward yourself, toward life, and toward your real day-to-day purpose. You have to have different objectives than the men around you. You have to have eternal objectives. You have to consider the spiritual stakes of inaction. You have to expand the reality of what retreat means from God's perspective. It requires you to partner with God in your life and make sure you are daily dialed in to the right channel—a secure connection to His Word and Spirit within you. Special Ops guys are great men, not because they possess amazing talent, but because they possess amazing commitment to the cause. This is what makes them brave. This is why they are the men of mythical proportions.

The message is simple: accept your assignments on earth, complete them, and become a true God's man.

You, my brother, are not a myth. Neither is your calling today, the calling to be one who leads. The message is simple: accept your assignments on earth, complete them, and become a true God's man. Remember the giver of the assignment, remember His words, and remember that He lives in you. To His Father He prayed, "I have brought you glory on earth by completing the work you gave me to do" (John 17:4).

Accomplish the work He has given you. Everything else is a diversion.

Just suit up and show up.

chapter 16

yes, you

If not you, who?

—Bill Bright

"Use me."

I whispered those words as I stared out the window of my hotel in Moscow. The year was 1985, I was nineteen years old, and I didn't know a lick of Russian.

I had culture shock.

Outside my window it was a drab, gloomy, and foreboding day, the titanic city with millions of trained atheists going about their lives, the Academy of Sciences building standing guard against guys like me foolish enough to invite the people of its country to put their faith in God. The next day I would be taking the elevator to the first floor, eating breakfast, and trying to lose myself in a sea of Soviet citizens, hoping to meet just one person. And ideally, that person would not be KGB.

To reach this moment, I'd spent three days sitting on my suitcase in the hallway of a train making my way from West Berlin, through Checkpoint Charlie, East Berlin, East Germany, Poland, and hundreds of miles of Soviet countryside. My buddies and I had escaped the night search by KGB at the border. Our materials were undiscovered, but the danger had put me on edge, and I was dog-tired.

My buddies and I had escaped the night search by KGB at the border. Our materials were undiscovered, but the danger had put me on edge, and I was dog-tired.

With closed borders and Christianity an official target of the government, 90 percent of the people in the Union of Soviet Socialist Republics had never heard the name of Jesus. Moscow was celebrating the Marxist Revolution—three generations of government-imposed godlessness. So that first night, I stood at my window, taking deep breaths, looking out over the city, and exhaling two words over and over: "Use me."

I will never forget the next morning, putting the two gospel tracts and the pocket New Testament I smuggled across the border into the back pockets of my Levi's and closing the door to my room. Another deep breath. *Here we go.*

At breakfast, my team of four men prayed looking at each other as if we were talking conversationally. We called it "talking to Dad," substituting *Dad* for *God* or *Father* as we prayed. We thought we were so sneaky.

A few minutes later, we caught a cab to Red Square and acted touristy, snapping a few pictures down side streets. We immediately caught the attention of six young Muscovite guys—or should I say *our jeans* caught their attention? We'd been warned about the black marketeers and in our training were encouraged to engage them. They spoke perfect English and were very engaging, and one seemed interested in something other than Levi's.

Smuggled into the Kingdom

The man was named Sasha. We sat on a bench next to the eternal flame of Russia—the symbol of Communist immortality—while a bride and groom dedicated their marriage to the service of the state. Ironically, as they were dedicating themselves to Communism, Sasha was about to be rescued from the same.

I felt no "anointing" as I pulled the tract from my back pocket. I was terrified I'd blow it. I robotically plowed my way through the *Four Spiritual Laws* in Russian (thank God he spoke English). As I read, instead of blowing me off, criticizing my butchering of his language, or asking me about my Sony Walkman, he hung on every word. It started to hit me that this was the first time Sasha had ever heard anyone talk to him about God.

I told him God's position of unconditional love. I told him about man's condition—separated from God and imperfect. I told him about God's forgiveness and provision of salvation through Jesus Christ and His death on the cross.

Then I flipped to the page with the two circles—one representing life without Christ, the other with Christ. Nervously, I said, "Point to the circle that best represents your life." He touched the circle without Christ. *Gulp.* "Which circle do you want to represent your life?" A pause.

(A pregnant pause.) And then, amazingly, I watched as his hand slowly floated over to the other circle. He tapped it a few times just to be sure.

Yes! Okay. The only thing left to do now is close this puppy and let him pray.

I read the prayer aloud and asked Sasha to repeat the words to God silently or aloud. I didn't hear anything, so after I finished reading, I asked if he had prayed. "I am asking Jesus into my heart right now," he said.

Oh, right. Rookie nerves!

After a few moments, Sasha looked up, his entire countenance changed, a broad smile invading his chiseled Russian face. In his heavy Russian accent, he explained his situation.

"When you explained to me...Jesus Christ, I knew that there was God."

"My parents are scientists, and they...er...told me ever since I was little boy that the government...er...hmm...could never say that there is not God. When you explained to me...Jesus Christ, I knew that there was God."

For a moment I was speechless, realizing I had absolutely nothing to do with what just transpired. The gospel was alive and operating at full power. God had been softening the soil, planting the seeds, cultivating Sasha's thoughts for years, and I was just a hired picker in the fields.

I quickly snapped out of it, remembering I needed to explain what his decision meant. The poor guy. Like a kindergarten teacher reading a fairy tale to her class, for the next couple of minutes I slowly read the rest of the booklet with him, explaining the impact of his decision. And like an engine starved for oil, he soaked up every scripture we read.

For the next three days we repeated these clandestine meetings and had more conversations about Sasha's new relationship with God. The dude was liquid-nitro ignited. I gave him triple portions of Bible, and every time, his plate was picked clean. His assimilation of the information under the pressure from his culture, the lack of resources, and the time crunch of my limited stay was truly supernatural. Finally, I took his name and number and promised him another American would come after me and get in touch with him for further meetings. I smuggled his contact information out, and he was successfully followed up.

Three weeks later, back at UCLA, I wandered into my fraternity house with just a passing glance at the mailboxes. Usually there was nothing there, but this time I had to put it in reverse at the sight of a letter in my slot. At first glance I was puzzled by the postmark: it was from the Netherlands. But inside there was another letter, this one with a Russian postmark! I opened it as if it were an excavated copy of the Ten Commandments—slowly, reverently.

> Kenny, brother, hallo! I've an excellent opportunity to bring you this letter. Here in Moscow I met a girl, she is from Holland and she will bring it to you. How are you? I'm fine. I love God and I believe. I believe so strong that there's no way back and God helps me. You are with me—I pray for you. Do you remember me? Long for hearin' from you.
>
> Sasha

It was incredible. And more incredible still, for my part, this silver thread of salvation embroidered on the dark cloth of atheistic Communism from halfway around the world began with two simple words: "Use me."

Use Me

Willing men inspire fear.

The one thing the devil fears more than any other is a God's man who is willing to say those two little words each day: "Use me." We especially grab his attention when God burdens us to begin inviting others to explore a relationship with Christ. He will stop at nothing to keep these two little words from ever being fused together in prayer. He needs to keep them separate in your life. Using other things is much better, he'll say. Using people, substances, credit cards, false motivations, feelings, is all great. Using them *now* is optimal.

Satan will stop at nothing to keep these two little words from ever being fused together in prayer.

If the devil can make God's man a dedicated user, occupying his life and mind with other things, we won't be available to be used by God. *So go on,* he'll say, *use, abuse, and blow a fuse!* Satan would love to decommission you, dishonorably discharge you, and destroy your availability.

The "me" part of that "use me" statement is potentially just as good a derailer (if not better). It diverts attention away from others and their need to know Christ and puts the focus on number one.

- "What about me?"
- "They're all following me!"
- "What's in it for me?"
- "Now they'll see me!"
- "Does the boss like me?"
- "How much money will it make me?"
- "What if they reject me?"
- "She wants me."

If the devil can't make you a user, he'll entice you to be self-absorbed and exploit your self-centered nature. When it comes to sharing your faith, being self-centered rather than other-centered makes him breathe a little easier. You will be so focused on yourself and your needs in the moment, it won't dawn on you that the other person might just be in your life for you to talk to about Christ. *C'mon,* Satan says, *why even risk it? What were you thinking, anyway? How does that help you? Forget about it.*

When it comes to sharing your faith, being self-centered rather than other-centered makes the devil breathe a little easier.

"Use me." Two little words—a verb and a pronoun. What's the big deal, you say? Put the two together, speak them sincerely to God, and mean it. In the natural realm, it may seem insignificant. But in the spiritual world there are huge repercussions.

- It means a soldier has been added—a marine, ready to be the first to fight for souls.
- It means God's man gets promoted from a bit player to the starting lineup.

- It means conversations about Christ and countless eternal consequences start spinning out into solid patterns.
- It means salvation, connection, and transformation of lives.
- It means forgiveness and healing.
- It means the game has changed forever.
- It means a warrior has been born and the gates of hell will not prevail against him.
- It means God's man has joined the ultimate battle line—the one of true consequence, the one that determines eternal destinies.
- It means a new asset is in play for the Enemy to contend with.

Willingness on the part of God's man to share the gospel is weapons-grade plutonium in spiritual warfare—the final ingredient that makes a nuclear impact possible. How is that, you say? Simple: telling someone else about the Lord requires humility and faith, the two most powerful agents of spiritual conductivity. God's power flows most deeply through you when you decide to leave the shores of safe, spiritual spin for the unpredictable rapids of witnessing.

Willingness on the part of God's man to share the gospel is weapons-grade plutonium in spiritual warfare—the final ingredient that makes a nuclear impact possible.

Your spiritual life comes full circle when you are willing to give away the same news you received and accepted yourself. You are owning the faith now instead of just leasing it when convenient. You have risked combining responsibility with willing availability to speak about Him. And once God's man experiences the power of God in this way, no other experience can compare. It is the ultimate risk-reward setup.

Ignition

Give the signal. Turn the key. Press the button. Release the power.

Men love the idea of ignition. Give them switches, keys, or buttons to press, flick on, or turn, that lead to noises, lights, power, or secret trapdoors. We love initiating sequences of things that blow up or blast off. At the moment of ignition, there's an excitement and a rush because we know a demonstration of power is going to follow. It is by design.

But imagine this: God wants you to *be* the ignition switch of His power by deciding to move the conversation over to Christ. According to Jesus, God's man can choose to experience the power of God by deciding to share his faith. Jesus put it this way to His guys: "You will receive power when the Holy Spirit comes on you; and you will be my witnesses in Jerusalem, and in all Judea and Samaria, and to the ends of the earth" (Acts 1:8). Whoa! Now that's a blast zone.

Stick to a simple testimony and gospel message. The Holy Spirit's job is to activate the words, multiply His power, and direct that energy toward the person we are talking to.

The only thing the boys were waiting for now was the ignition switch of the Holy Spirit. It came at Pentecost where they all went nuclear, boldly sharing the gospel without fear (note: for the full picture read Acts 2–4 and take a look at the promise fulfilled). The point to ponder is this: the power is given and the power is experienced by God's man when he opens his mouth for the King.

The apostle Paul ignited this insight into how God's man experiences the release of God's power in and through him: "When I came to you, brothers, I did not come with eloquence or superior wisdom as I proclaimed to you the testimony about God. For I resolved to know nothing while I was with you except Jesus Christ and him crucified. I came to you in weakness and fear, and with much trembling. My message and my preaching were not with wise and persuasive words, but with a demonstration of the Spirit's power, so that your faith might not rest on men's wisdom, but on God's power" (1 Corinthians 2:1–5). He showed up. He was willing to open his mouth. And the rest was on God.

The point to ponder here is this: for God's man, intellectual knowledge is not the issue. "I don't know enough" is no longer in play. In fact, the less we claim to know, the more raw and honest the message, the more power flows through us. Stick to a simple testimony and gospel message. The Holy Spirit's job is to activate the words, multiply His power, and direct that energy toward the person we are talking to.

I can relate to Paul's fear and his experience of the power of God invading another's world through him. I felt it when I stood face to face with a six-foot-six fraternity brother God burdened me to invite to an outreach at UCLA. I felt it with my neighbor, Dan, for whom I had prayed for years and then invited to church the day he got his cancer diagnosis. I felt it witnessing to my daughter's soccer coach. I felt it when the other passengers on the plane overheard me witnessing to an older lady from Texas. I felt it when I wanted to talk about heaven with my mom on her deathbed.

What exactly did I feel? I felt brief panic turn to power when I stepped out in faith. In fact, it always feels that way for me. In each of these instances, I felt like a Special Forces guy being dropped from the sky into a situation. I might make hundreds of jumps in a lifetime, but each one still comes with jitters before the jump. You believe the chute will open, and when you jump out of the plane, you have full faith that it can carry you safely into the mission.

But the question is: *Will it?*

God's men should expect our initiative to ignite His power and the gospel to deliver a powerful blow to the heart.

God's man has an even greater promise. The power is always going to be there when he jumps into the mission of rescuing people. He will be carried, supported, and improved whether or not the person receives Christ. He will feel the power and energy that only come after obedience.

More times than not when sharing my faith, I have experienced something even greater than personal satisfaction—the power of salvation. Each of those people mentioned and hundreds more have proven to me that God's power is waiting to be unleashed if we move against fear and reason to share our Lord with someone. That is the real eyeopener.

The goal is to get to this place of responsibility, availability, and all-important expectancy. God's men should expect our initiative to ignite His power and the gospel to deliver a powerful blow to the heart. With such faith in the gospel's power, our small role becomes clear, our message less important, and we learn to confidently trust in its ability over our own. In fact, when we risk sharing our faith frequently, our experience of God's power enables us to say, "I am not ashamed of the gospel, because it is the power of God for the salvation of everyone who believes" (Romans 1:16).

This is where every God's man gets to be, in every facet of life. The problem is most men hedge their bets, stop short. We don't experience the confidence until we risk sharing the gospel to get the results.

My point: risk sharing your faith more. God Himself will show up; He guarantees it. And the next time won't feel so strange. And the next time, even less, and so on and so on.

Game on?

Are You Praying for Open Doors?

God's man is proactive on the gospel front. He's an infantryman hungry for some action, praying for assignments. If you are in a men's group, your group should make evangelism a part of your group culture and covenant. If you have an accountability partner, you should load in an accountability question for evangelism alongside of the sexual-temptation question (try publicly witnessing to the lady you're tempted by and see what happens!). Few men I work with are naturally aggressive in sharing their faith. Most of us need to train up and into spiritual confidence first. We have to *own* it.

God's man is proactive on the gospel front. He's an infantryman hungry for some action, praying for assignments.

The key to developing God's purpose for evangelism starts here. We must be convinced that this is His priority for our lives. God commands that we go and make disciples (see Matthew 28:18–20). Next, we need to pray for opportunities and be mindful that God will layer us into situations—

some obvious and some not so obvious—that call us to share our testimony and the gospel on His time. Last, we are to proactively pursue, encourage, and sharpen each other in witnessing.

As we risk building a lifestyle of evangelism through prayer and then practice, we will begin to see the custom-built opportunities God has already laid out. Prayer will be the key at each step of the process:

> Devote yourselves to prayer, being watchful and thankful. And pray for us, too, that God may open a door for our message, so that we may proclaim the mystery of Christ, for which I am in chains. Pray that I may proclaim it clearly, as I should. Be wise in the way you act toward outsiders; make the most of every opportunity. Let your conversation be always full of grace, seasoned with salt, so that you may know how to answer everyone." (Colossians 4:2–6)

Great evangelism is always:

- started by prayer
- secured by prayer
- supported by prayer
- steered and guided by prayer
- successful and fruitful by prayer

So who was the last person you prayed about sharing your faith with?

Whether you are a veteran or just now blasting off toward the challenge, praying the following prayer on a regular basis will help form your heart for reaching others for Christ.

Lord Jesus,

Thank You for reaching out to me. I want to be God's man in reaching others with the good news of Your great love. I ask You to open my heart to people's eternal condition and future, to open my ears to hear the needs around me and meet them, to lead me to the specific people You want me to talk to, to open the doors and opportunities for me to share with them, to open my mouth to share clearly, sincerely, and openly about how You came into my life and changed me. Thank You that I have what I ask, because I ask according to Your will. In the name of Jesus I pray, Amen.

If you prayed that and meant it, watch out. You've just said to God: "Use me." He's going to bring those people. It's game-on time for the kingdom!

Imagine the footholds of the Enemy that will be taken back, lives saved, relationships transformed, generations affected because you'll open your mouth and let God make something happen.

All you have to do is go through those doors and ignite the power.

Whoa! What a ride.

Special note: When God answers your prayer and uses you to touch someone for Christ, please tell me so I can celebrate with you. E-mail your story to kennyl@everymanministries.com. And if you would like to get ahold of resources that will help you share your faith, log on to www.everymanministries.com and click the *Risk* book icon on the home page.

chapter 17

bet it all

Only those who risk going too far can possibly find out how far they can go.

—T. S. Eliot

Mohammed Odeh Al-Rehaief (pronounced "all-ra-heef") did not consider himself a great man. He was a lawyer in the city of Nasiriya, and his wife was a nurse at the local hospital; his children were well provided for and his family well known.

As a Shiite, Al-Rehaief was elated at the American offensive under way in his hometown. During the first Iraq war, Saddam had brutally crushed a Shiite rebellion in the south where he lived through purges, murder, and savage oppression. People had disappeared without a trace. And Al-Rehaief had seen it all firsthand. The prospect of freedom—for him, his family, and his people—was finally becoming a reality. The familiar fear was finally lifting, the terror turning to hope.

He carried this hope in his heart the day he went to visit his wife at the hospital. It was ten days into the war, the conflict in Nasiriya was intensifying, and he was coming to take his wife and family away from the fighting. He was walking down a hallway when he heard Iraqi officers screaming at someone in a nearby room.

Without thinking, he went in and saw three men standing over a woman in a hospital bed. The badly injured woman was being beaten by what looked like a militia officer for the *fedayeen* (Saddam's secret police). Al-Rehaief instantly knew two things. One, the woman he saw was an American soldier. Two, she was going to die if something wasn't done.

Why risk everything for someone he didn't even know?

He knew how these guys operated. In the seconds following his hasty exit from the room, the course of his life changed. Al-Rehaief decided to risk everything to help her.

His exploits in the hours and days following were widely reported and well documented.

- He decided in the hospital that he would tell the Americans about this woman. He didn't even know her name (Jessica Lynch).
- He made his way through a raging gun battle to the outskirts of Nasiriya and faced being shot by American soldiers in order to tell them about Lynch.
- After intense questioning by American troops he was sent *back* to gather information and logistics that would be critical for the rescue.

- On his return to the Americans through "no man's land," he was nearly killed by a bomb that blew up the car behind his. Shrapnel from the explosion pierced his car and punctured his left eye. He lost his vision in the eye.
- The car that exploded belonged to the Iraqi secret police who were chasing Al-Rehaief.
- The detailed information he delivered to the Americans allowed a Special Forces team to rescue Lynch.

What in the world was this guy thinking? Wasn't he afraid? Why in the world did he do it? Why risk everything for someone he didn't even know?

A *Newsweek* interview conducted after the rescue uncovered the thoughts and fears driving Al-Rehaief as he entered and miraculously made it out of the end of this amazing gauntlet. His responses were truly remarkable.

- "The American troops, they crossed oceans, they left families, their kids, their loved ones behind and they came to help us—putting their lives in danger. They took a big risk doing that. Naturally, I should help them. So I put my life in danger."
- "It was my duty to help her. I looked at her like she was a savior for us. We were living under a cruel dictatorship."
- "What I did put my life and my daughter's life and my wife's life on the line. But I believe it was worth it."
- "I didn't fear for myself; I feared for my family."
- "Death was everywhere, you didn't know when you were going to get killed. So I was expecting nothing. I didn't know if I was going to be alive or dead. I was living minute to minute and these minutes were a trip toward the unknown."
- "It was the right thing to do."[1]

That last one knocks me out. The fact that he can say these words! "It was the right thing to do," and he *did something* about it. In his own mind, he made a calculated decision to go against his fears and feelings. He erred on the side of daring over the side of caution for all the right reasons.

In Al-Rehaief we learn not only about a great man who did a great thing, we see a parable of how men are moved beyond self-preservation to greatness. We see the anatomy of the thoughts and actions of a true hero.

- *He reciprocated with risk.* He saw men and women risking their lives for him and felt a responsibility to risk back. *That* was the right thing to do. *He made it personal.*
- *He reacted right away.* He felt a deep gratitude when he looked at Jessica Lynch. He let it hit him emotionally. It was an emotional reaction at first. Then he let it move from his heart *past his head* and to his behavior in *real time.* That is, in time to help. *He didn't overthink it.*
- *He released the outcomes.* He acted on principle and did not require guaranteed outcomes. Death. Life. Success. Failure. *He was going regardless.*
- *He remembered his duty.* He did not excuse himself from his responsibility to act. His inner constitution prevailed over fears or feelings that might amend or bend it. *He lived out his values.*
- *He ran into the dark.* He did not let the unknowns stop him. He leapt, not knowing if a net would appear. He could not see where his risk was going to take him. *He discovered the way one step at a time.*
- *He resisted retreat.* He showed his commitment by going back *twice.* He exposed himself repeatedly and at a higher chance of death. *He did not look for a back door so he could back off.*
- *He relied on a higher purpose.* He connected helping a woman live to helping the cause of liberty in his own life and for his people. These

> purposes provided courage and confidence to risk it all. They dignified and justified his efforts. *He fortified and strengthened his resolve by uniting his actions to a greater cause.*

When confronted with the opportunity, Al-Rehaief was a personally motivated and grateful responder who was unconditionally committed to his values and his cause. He even lost an eye to prove it. His story will be told and retold by his great-great-great-grandchildren.

God's Man Risks

Taking risks for God leads to a richer relationship with Him. More important, when we push the envelope of His promises, we get to personally see His purposes worked out in the world.

Think Abraham's emergency relocation process. Think Joshua and the march-and-blow strategy for Jericho. Think Noah's shipping order. Think of Joshua getting a million people to the other side of the river, only to start multiple wars based on a promise. Think of David teeing off on Goliath. Think Elijah calling out the prophets of Baal. Think Daniel refusing steak and asking for veggies. Think Stephen before the Sanhedrin. Think Jesus in the Garden of Gethsemane. Think [your name here] plus [risk issue].

He could not see where his risk was going to take him. He discovered the way one step at a time.

Every guy was God's man. Every guy was tested. Every man stood alone. Every man risked trusting God and prevailed. The common denominators of these risk-taking experiences were:

- All accepted their assignments.
- All required trust in God's way over their way.
- All followed a higher purpose—mostly unknown to them until later.
- All looked forward to heavenly reward over earthly approval.
- All were offered no guarantees, only promises from God that He would help them.
- All experienced internal conflict.
- All went against the odds, their feelings, fears, doubts, culture, and circumstances.
- All experienced a loss, some through disapproval, others through stoning or crucifixion.
- All were recognized and rewarded generously by God.
- All have a legacy.

These are the big hitters, the Hall of Famers, the recognized risk takers. But it would be a mistake to think that slaying a giant, crossing a river, being killed as a martyr, or calling down fire is all that garners God's attention. The Bible makes it clear that any decision to put God's agenda ahead of yours, ahead of money, ahead of feelings, titles, and desires pleases God.

The Word ahead of the world. The gospel ahead of gurus. Self-sacrifice over selfishness. Relationships over busyness.

The Word ahead of the world. The gospel ahead of gurus. Self-sacrifice over selfishness. Relationships over busyness. These are also the risks that are recognized, recorded, and rewarded by God. The Bible says that any loss related to these risks taken for Him and His purposes—whether literal, emotional, relational, circumstantial, financial, or whatever-al—will be compensated in full by God.

Jesus made sure to get His guys ready for living a life shaped by risk early in the game.

> Blessed are you who are poor,
> for yours is the kingdom of God.
> Blessed are you who hunger now,
> for you will be satisfied.
> Blessed are you who weep now,
> for you will laugh.
> Blessed are you when men hate you,
> when they exclude you and insult you
> and reject your name as evil, because of the Son of Man.
>
> Rejoice in that day and leap for joy, because great is your reward in heaven. (Luke 6:20–23)

Living as God's men would involve sacrifice. But Jesus wanted to make triple-dog sure that His guys had His official guarantee: the score would be settled, and they would be elated at the return. The investment had to be made *now;* everything would be left on the field. They would be called to risk putting their entire lives in play for the kingdom.

The investment had to be made now; *everything would be left on the field. They would be called to risk putting their entire lives in play for the kingdom*

And the rewards would all come to them, some on earth but mostly in heaven. Every God's man is called to arrange his life to accommodate increasing levels of spiritual risk.

Do that, and your first moments in heaven will be very good. For you, but mostly for God.

Conservative, Moderate, or Aggressive

When I look at Jesus's words to His guys about risking it all for Him, I am reminded of a brochure I received from a financial-services company. It had a simple graph profiling my level of comfort with financial risk. I could fit one of three categories based on the level of risk I could tolerate: conservative, moderate, or aggressive.

It was all so simple and straightforward. Most financial advisors would suggest you split up your financial pie among many different types of investments, though they're quick to remind you not to expect double-digit percentages in the return column. The more time you have before retirement, they say, the less aggressive you need to be. The less time you have before retirement, the more aggressive you may need to be to build the wealth you need.

Then in a flash, it hit me: Jesus put the same scenario to His guys. But the currency was not denari or shekels; it was their lives. Also, there was no moderate category—no middle ground to spiritual significance and impact. Risk it and gain more. Play it safe and lose it. Only one profitable category—aggressive risk. Jesus knew that their time here on earth was short and that they would need to fearlessly invest in the kingdom to build true spiritual wealth in the time allotted.

The spiritually safe life is ultimately the most dangerous of all. How dangerous? Paul put it to the Corinthians this way: if you risk nothing for your faith on earth, you waste your grace.

> By the grace God has given me, I laid a foundation as an expert builder, and someone else is building on it. But each one should be careful how he builds. For no one can lay any foundation other than the one already laid, which is Jesus Christ. If any man builds on this foundation using gold, silver, costly stones, wood, hay or straw, his work will be shown for what it is, because the Day will bring it to light. It will be revealed with fire, and the fire will test the quality of each man's work. If what he has built survives, he will receive his reward. If it is burned up, he will suffer loss; he himself will be saved, but only as one escaping through the flames. (1 Corinthians 3:10–15)

God is looking for aggressive spiritual investors, guaranteeing killer returns on investment. There is no moderate column for growing your spiritual portfolio. You must risk. God risked sending His Son, investing His blood, and generously giving forgiveness and grace for you so that He could seek a return. For God's man it means this: He wants to multiply His grace, mercy, and love toward you into new convictions, new character, new choices, and new conduct. And He wants to see increasing levels of health in your relationships with Him and others.

The only solid risk for God's man, as Paul so matter-of-factly tells us, is Jesus Christ. You cannot live for anything or anyone else and expect a return that outlasts your life on earth. The good energy, the big choices, the core relationships, and the productive capacities are our precious offerings we risk placing in God's hands for His multiplication.

The critical mistake so many make is carving out only a small part of their life portfolio for Him, investing in other things that produce no return. In other words, they waste Christ's sacrifice on themselves.

The whole point of this book, of reading story after story of men risking, is to show you how men are made to risk, to encourage you to be an aggressive risk taker for God, and above all to get you to act on what you know God is calling you to do.

There are two ways to go in your life of faith. Which road would the little boy in you take?

"What is it?" you ask. Here's a clue: whatever makes you swallow big. My friend Lee Strobel puts it this way:

> When we take a risk, we're stretching beyond what we think are our limits in order to reach for a goal. Inevitably, that involves overcoming some sort of fear—fear of the unknown, of physical harm, of failure, of humiliation, even of success. And it involves adventure.
>
> When I was in college a friend often lent me his Kawasaki motorcycle, which was primarily designed for off-road use. When I'd ride thirty miles an hour down the smooth residential streets toward campus, it was safe but boring. Wind whipped my hair but my heart didn't quiver. However, when I'd go zipping off the road, through tall weeds, down twisting dirt trails, dodging trees and bushes, around boulders, and up steep inclines—places where I was facing some risk—that was exciting.
>
> The same could be said for living a life of faith. It's when we overcome our fears and take spiritual risks that we really experience the adventure of Christianity. Jesus said, in effect, that those who

> risk their whole life for him will find it, but those who hang on to their life—those who shrink back from risk—will be the losers.[2]

There are two ways to go in your life of faith: smooth, residential, safe, and boring; or off-road, twisting, riskier, and exciting. Which road would the little boy in you take?

Some of us look for any excuse to open up the throttle, push our bodies past their limits, and live on the edge. That is from God, my brother! Jesus wanted that life for you, and He is making *Himself* your excuse to live the dream and love the extreme. Your energy and willingness to invest it for Christ is not slipping God's watchful eye. He's hoping you'll cross the line in those areas of your life that will most stretch you to be His man—right now.

The question for you is this: *Can God be trusted?*

He Earned It

Roger Bannister broke a barrier some thought would never be broken—the four-minute mile. When he reflected on his titanic athletic achievement, he said, "The man who can drive himself further once the pain starts is the man who will win." Few men can say this because few men have driven themselves beyond their pain threshold to break barriers and secure a victory. We can risk trusting what Roger said because he embodied what he said. We consider the man, consider his words, and we believe him. He earned our trust.

Jesus Christ didn't set a record time, He stopped time (check your calendar). He didn't defeat a clock, He secured an eternity. He didn't shed tears of victory; instead He shed His dignity. He didn't make the headlines that fateful day, but He was looking ahead to see your day. He didn't complain once the pain started; He invited more when He could have stopped it. He was not applauded for His deed; He was abandoned and sentenced to bleed. Jesus drove Himself further and harder than any man who ever lived, endured the greatest pain any man ever endured. Why?

"If you try to keep your life for yourself, you will lose it. But if you give up your life for my sake and for the sake of the Good News, you will find true life" (Mark 8:35, NLT). No man can ever make a request like this because no man has risked more for you than your Savior. Could we risk trusting and acting on what He said if He hadn't embodied what He said? We consider the man, consider His words, and we believe Him. More specifically, God's man, we give up our lives completely for Him. He earned our unlimited trust. We can bet it all.

We can't look up at the Man on the cross and lose in our quest to throw spiritual caution and fear to the wind. Instead we can only be strengthened in our resolve to risk progressively more and more. In fact, the longer we look at Him up there, the more dangerous we become for the kingdom. We join the ranks of men who saw Him from a distance and risked, men who walked with Him up close, and men who through the centuries endangered others with kingdom-splitting conviction.

If you are to bet it all, study the Man who risked it all.

> Keep your eyes on *Jesus,* who both began and finished this race we're in. Study how he did it. Because he never lost sight of where he was headed—that exhilarating finish in and with God—he could put up with anything along the way: Cross, shame, whatever. And now he's

> *there,* in the place of honor, right alongside God. When you find yourselves flagging in your faith, go over that story again, item by item, that long litany of hostility he plowed through. *That* will shoot adrenaline into your souls! (Hebrews 12:2–3, MSG)

Every risk we take for Him, He earned and then some. We will never be able to pay Him back. But we can show our gratitude by remembering the greatest risk ever taken and responding gratefully with some risk-taking of our own. He will show us His stripes one day—the scars. The ones on His body that healed us and saved us. He will show us because scars tell stories. Scars prove your story. Scars remind. Scars show the cost. Scars motivate. Scars inspire. And scars are beautiful.

Scars tell you that a Man was not playing it safe.

And that Man lives in you.

notes

Chapter 4

1. John Foxe, *The New Foxe's Book of Martyrs* (North Brunswick, NJ: Bridge-Logos, 1997), 16.
2. Foxe, *Martyrs,* 14.
3. John Piper, *Don't Waste Your Life* (Wheaton, IL: Crossway, 2003), 87.

Chapter 5

1. Jim Muzikowski, *Safe at Home* (Grand Rapids: Zondervan, 2001), 42.

Chapter 6

1. Stuart Briscoe, *The One Year Book of Devotions for Men* (Wheaton, IL: Tyndale, 2000).

Chapter 7

1. Laurence Gonzales, "Hooked," *Men's Health,* October 2005, 190.

Chapter 8

1. Donald Miller, *Blue Like Jazz* (Nashville: Thomas Nelson, 2003), 189–92.

Chapter 10

1. Stu Weber, *All the King's Men* (Sisters, OR: Multnomah, 1998), 162.
2. This study is quoted from Steve Farrar, *Finishing Strong* (Sisters, OR: Multnomah, 2000).

Chapter 11

1. Chad Bonham, comp., "Head's Trip," *New Man,* September–October 2005, 10–11.
2. John Owen, "Of the Mortification of Sin in Believers," *Triumph Over Temptation: The Challenge of Personal Godliness,* ed. James M. Houston (Colorado Springs, CO: Victor, 2005), 216–17.

Chapter 13

1. "Ebola Hemorrhagic Fever Information Packet," U.S. Department of Health and Human Services, Centers for Disease Control and Prevention, 2002 Special Pathogens Branch, http://www.cdc.gov/ncidod/dvrd/spb/mnpages/ebola.pdf.

Chapter 14

1. Malcom Gladwell, *Blink* (New York: Little, Brown and Company, 2005), 97–98.

Chapter 17

1. Adam Piore, " 'Why I Risked My Life': Mohammed Odeh Al-Rehaief Discusses His Role in the Rescue of Jessica Lynch, His New Home in the United States and How He Sees the Future of Iraq," *Newsweek Web Exclusive,* October 29, 2003, http://msnbc.msn.com/id/ 3339596/site/newsweek/ (accessed November 30, 2005).
2. Lee Strobel, *God's Outrageous Claims* (Grand Rapids: Zondervan, 1997), 199–200.

about the author

Kenny Luck is the men's pastor at Saddleback Church in Lake Forest, California. He is also the founder and president of Every Man Ministries, which helps churches worldwide develop and grow healthy men's communities.

He is a winner of the ECPA Platinum Award, and he has authored and coauthored seventeen books, including *Every Man, God's Man; Every Young Man, God's Man;* and the Every Man Bible studies from the bestselling Every Man series. Kenny is a featured columnist for *New Man* magazine and a frequent guest for national media outlets as an expert on men's issues.

Kenny is a graduate of UCLA, where he met his wife, Chrissy. They have three children—Cara, Ryan, and Jenna—and live in Trabuco Canyon, California. He plays in a men's soccer league, enjoys mountain biking, and loves playing flag football on Thanksgiving mornings.